DAVID HINTON

I CHING

David Hinton has translated many works of classical Chinese poetry, earning him wide acclaim for creating compelling contemporary poems that convey the actual texture and density of the originals. He is the first person in more than a century to translate the five seminal masterworks of Chinese philosophy. He has received fellowships from the Guggenheim Foundation, the National Endowment for the Arts, and the National Endowment for the Humanities, and has won both major awards given for translation in the United States. Most recently, he was awarded the Thornton Wilder Prize for lifetime achievement from the American Academy of Arts and Letters.

ALSO BY DAVID HINTON

ESSAYS

Existence: A Story

Hunger Mountain: A Field Guide to Mind and Landscape

POETRY

Fossil Sky

TRANSLATIONS

The Late Poems of Wang An-shih

The Four Chinese Classics

Classical Chinese Poetry: An Anthology

The Selected Poems of Wang Wei

The Mountain Poems of Meng Hao-jan

Mountain Home: The Wilderness Poetry of Ancient China

The Mountain Poems of Hsieh Ling-yün

Tao Te Ching

The Selected Poems of Po Chü-i

The Analects

Mencius

Chuang Tzu: The Inner Chapters

The Late Poems of Meng Chiao

The Selected Poems of Li Po

The Selected Poems of T'ao Ch'ien

The Selected Poems of Tu Fu

I CHING

3 5 7 9 10 8 6 4

I CHING

THE BOOK OF CHANGE

TRANSLATED BY

DAVID HINTON

FARRAR, STRAUS AND GIROUX   NEW YORK

Farrar, Straus and Giroux
18 West 18th Street, New York 10011

The Library of Congress has cataloged the hardcover edition as follows:
Yi jing. English.
    I Ching : the book of change / translated by David Hinton. — First edition.
       pages   cm
    ISBN 978-0-374-22090-7 (hardcover) — ISBN 978-1-4668-4852-8 (e-book)
    1. Yi jing.   I. Hinton, David, 1954– translator.

PL2478 .D38 2015
299.5'1282—dc23

                                                        2014046629

Paperback ISBN: 978-0-374-53642-8
5 7 9 10 8 6 4
Our books may be purchased in bulk for promotional, educational, or business use.
Please contact your local bookseller or the Macmillan Corporate and Premium Sales
Department at 1-800-221-7945, extension 5442, or by e-mail at
MacmillanSpecialMarkets@macmillan.com.

www.fsgbooks.com
www.twitter.com/fsgbooks • www.facebook.com/fsgbooks

CONTENTS

INTRODUCTION

Primal emptiness separated into heaven and earth. That's how it all began. Before long, a pair of dragons emerged from Bright-Prosperity Mountain: Root-Breath and Lady She-Voice. Now, dragons in ancient China embodied the awesome force of change. A dragon was in constant transformation, writhing through all creation and all destruction, shaping itself into the ten thousand things tumbling through their traceless transformations. So perhaps the appearance of these dragons was the beginning of the ever-changing diversity of things we know as the Cosmos. The legend doesn't say. Root-Breath and Lady She-Voice were dragons, but dragons with human heads. They became the first couple, husband and wife, and Lady She-Voice gave birth to humankind. So you see, we are descended from dragons: we have dragon hearts pumping dragon blood, dragon minds thinking dragon thoughts.

It was Root-Breath, our first-ancestor, who created the hexagrams. More dragon than human, his thoughts were almost indistinguishable from natural process itself, so when he shaped them into the hexagrams, those strange dragon-graphs expressed all phenomena in the endless process of change. Language is how we represent change, reality in its dynamic process of transformation. And it grows out of change. Hexagrams are the first stage in that emergence of language from change, that folding of the Cosmos around onto itself to name and describe itself. They are the most ancient form of language in this sense. Part dragon language, part human, they represent the movement of change at a more fundamental level than our languages can.

Root-Breath's hexagrams were made up of six lines, each of which could be either a solid *yang* (male) line (—) or a divided *yin* (female) line (– –), thereby representing the two complementary cosmic principles whose dynamic interaction produces the process of change. And these lines were alive. Like dragons and the Cosmos itself, the hexagram lines were in constant transformation—*yang* becoming *yin*, and *yin*, *yang*—creating different hexagrams, each of which is defined by its particular configuration of *yang* and *yin*. So there are sixty-four hexagrams—every possible six-line combination of *yang* and *yin* lines—and these combinations describe every possible configuration in the process of change. The sixty-four hexagrams make up the actual text of the *I Ching*: *I* (Change) + *Ching* (Classic) = *The Classic of Change* or *The Book of Change*. *The Book of Change* and change itself: they emerged together at the beginning of things. And the first two hexagrams return us to that beginning:

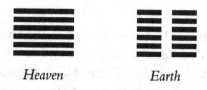

Heaven   *Earth*

As they express all phenomena past, present, and future, the hexagrams contained the secrets of civilization, too. Applying those secrets, Root-Breath taught people how to hunt and fish, how to keep livestock and cook with fire. He was the first emperor, and the ancient emperors that followed also understood the secrets contained in his hexagrams. Using the hexagrams, they taught people about bow and arrow, plow and boat, pottery and markets, carts and buildings, and finally: writing. And so it makes sense, because it grew out of the hexagrams, that writing would be in the form of pictograms representing reality with all immediacy.

All of this time, the earth was alive with geologic transformation. Much later, it was covered by a flood, and another great emperor rescued the people by raising up mountains and carving out rivers to drain floodwaters away. Maybe it happened because writing was invented. Or maybe it was because we had grown too far from our dragon ancestors. No one knows. But somehow, after the floodwaters drained away, legendary emperors were no more and we lost our ability to decipher the primeval language of hexagrams. And so eventually, sages began writing descriptions and interpretations and evocations of the hexagrams, trying to articulate the possibilities opened by those dragon-graphs. It was a kind of philosophical storytelling. First they gave the hexagrams names and evocative interpretations. Then they described and interpreted the individual lines within the configuration of each hexagram. Eventually, they described and interpreted the trigrams, the top and bottom halves of the hexagrams. And because those original hexagram interpretations were so mysterious, they added elaborations on those interpretations. These first levels of elaboration were hardly less primal and mysterious than the hexagrams themselves. Indeed, they seem to *establish* the mysteries of the original hexagrams, rather than *explain* them. They were, we might now say, poetry (indeed, much of this text is rhymed in the original). These are the layers of the *I Ching* presented here, perhaps the most ancient of all Chinese texts, full of poetry and mysterious philosophy, alive somehow outside of time, both primal and postmodern at once.

Several layers of later explanation were eventually added to the text; but unlike the original linguistic layers that function as literary text, these later layers feel like secondary commentary. Still, they were included in the book; and with that, the canonical *I Ching* was complete sometime around the third century B.C.E. As the centuries passed, schemes for interpreting that canonical *I Ching* multiplied into the thousands, led by Confucian moralizing with its interpretive fantasies, which were also applied to the ancient *Book of Songs* (*Shih Ching*), where the simplest and most transparent folk songs were turned into rigorous allegories for proper ethical and political behavior. This was part of a widespread desire to use the *I Ching* for practical purposes, which began very early, for the book was seen from ancient times as a divination text that could instruct us about how best to proceed in a given situation.

After the floodwaters drained away, there arose the Hsia dynasty, about which little is known, followed by the Shang dynasty (1766–1040 B.C.E.). In the Shang theocratic worldview, all things were created and controlled by Shang Ti ("Celestial Lord"), an all-powerful monotheistic deity not unlike the Judeo-Christian god. Events could also be influenced by dead ancestors who were powerful in the spirit world. And so, divination practices assumed that fate was determined by outside forces. When the Shang emperors grew tyrannical, the dynasty was replaced by the Chou dynasty (1040–223 B.C.E.). Now, Shang Ti was the high ancestor of the Shang rulers, and he provided them with a transcendental source of legitimacy and power. In order to justify their rule, the Chou rulers reinvented Shang Ti as the impersonal "heaven," thus ending the Shang claim to legitimacy by lineage; and then the Chou rulers proclaimed that the right to rule depended upon the "Mandate of Heaven": once a ruler becomes unworthy, heaven withdraws its mandate and bestows it on another. This was a major event in Chinese history: the first investment of power with an ethical imperative.

The *I Ching* was projected into this historical transition when later ages attributed the early textual levels to major figures in the transition, attributions that are almost certainly false, but did in fact shape the culture's development over millennia. According to this cultural legend, Emperor Wen ("cultured": c. 1150 B.C.E.) gave the hexagrams names and composed the initial Statements (appearing in this translation immediately beneath the hexagram title) while imprisoned for giving honest advice and criticism to the Shang dynasty's last tyrannical emperor. Wen was the sage ruler of the neighboring state of Chou, and he laid the foundation for the overthrow of the Shang by his son Emperor Wu ("martial"). Wen's other son, the Duke of Chou, was a great philosopher and poet: the inventor of the Mandate of Heaven concept and the author of many poems in the *Book of Songs*. He is said to have written the evocative interpretations for the individual lines of each hexagram. And it was said that the other layers of the original text were written half a millennium later by Confucius (551–479 B.C.E.), the seminal philosopher who created the political philosophy that was a secularized replacement for the Shang dynasty's theocratic system.

The transformation of the source of creation and order from an otherworldly sky god, Shang Ti, to an impersonal heaven was soon superseded in the philosophical world when heaven became an entirely empirical phenomenon: the generative cosmological principle that drives change. Although heaven is sometimes referred to alone in this sense, an echo of its earlier use as an impersonal deity, it is really only half of a whole. The other half is earth. The two together, in their interaction as cosmic *yang* (male) and *yin* (female), generate the Cosmos as an ongoing process. This heaven is 天, which also means simply "sky," and its complement, earth, is 土. This set of terms emphasizes the physical entities that we know so well, but also includes the cosmological principles. 天 and 土 occur routinely in the *I Ching*, but there is another pair of terms that reverses the emphasis: 乾 and 坤. These terms, the titles of the first two hexagrams, emphasize heaven as the active generative force of the Cosmos and earth as the receptive generative force. It is their ceaseless interaction that generates the process of change. The two might be read as "Creative" and "Receptive," but in this translation both pairs of terms are translated as "heaven and earth," for this suggests the cosmological dimensions that return us always to the originary moment when heaven and earth appeared out of primal emptiness.

This heaven-and-earth Cosmos is also the Cosmos of our immediate experience, and if we don't think of heaven and earth as mere abstractions, we can see that heaven and earth are indeed an accurate description of the physical reality in which we live. The generative life-supporting reality of earth requires the infusion of energies from heaven: sunlight, rain, snow, air. We dwell in our everyday lives at the origin place where this vital intermingling of heaven and earth takes place, at the center of a dynamic cocoon of cosmic energy, an all-encompassing generative present. We are rarely aware of this wondrous fact; but for the ancients, this awareness shaped everyday existence.

Once Shang Ti was transformed into the cosmological process of change, divination too was transformed. Rather than fortune-telling, an appeal to deities who control fate, it assumes that change unfolds organically, things unfolding according to their own inner principles, and that all those things in the process of change are related. So if we can discern where exactly we are in that organic unfolding, we might discern how to proceed for the best result. This is how divination works in the *I Ching*, and it reveals a remarkable transformation. In the Shang, people didn't experience themselves as substantially different from spirits, for the human realm was simply an extension of the spirit realm. In this, the Shang system was hardly different from the Judeo-Christian West. But the *I Ching* assumes a much more primal experience, one that apparently survived outside the mythology of power that supported the Shang. In this experience, we are entirely earthly, an integral part of the unfolding of change.

The *I Ching*'s assumption that one can act to influence one's fate also reflects this transformation. Rather than simply obey political power and implore the spirits to shape your fate in positive ways, the question of wisdom arises, and the empowerment that wisdom offers: act wisely and good things happen, act unwisely and bad things happen. The *I Ching* hexagrams embody change in a schematic form, so they allow us to locate ourselves in the unfolding of change. This requires that you use either "shaman-flower" (yarrow) stems or coins to perform a "chance" procedure (see "How to Consult the I Ching," p. 135). We call it a chance procedure, but it is in fact a distilled moment in the process of change, and so it allows you to find the hexagram relevant to your situation. Then, because all change is interrelated, the *I Ching* is able to offer in its mysterious way advice about how to proceed. Or so the story goes.

Ancient China's intellectuals—artists, writers, thinkers, monks—were skeptical and empirical by nature, and they saw the *I Ching* not primarily as a divination text, but as a wisdom text: the most ancient source of the philosophical system that shaped their experience. And in fact, the hexagrams don't so much tell fortunes in any precise way as describe the various trends or forces that guide change. Seen in this light, the *I Ching* is a proto-Taoist philosophical text describing in rudimentary and fragmentary form the fundamental picture of the Cosmos that is described more fully in the seminal Taoist texts to follow: the *Tao Te Ching* (c. 500 B.C.E.) and the *Chuang Tzu* (c. 300). This is the *I Ching* that was a fundamental influence on China's artists and intellectuals, those creators of Chinese culture. That is to say, it is the *I Ching* that profoundly influenced the shape of Chinese culture as it evolved over the millennia, and it is how the text is presented in this translation.

The *Tao Te Ching* is a compilation of fragments from an oral tradition that stretches back to the beginnings of human culture in China. The *I Ching* seems also to include many such fragments, and its ultimate sources apparently lie at least as far back. Its mysterious utterances and form certainly justify the myth describing it as a philosophy that emerged even before language. But myth or no, it would seem to be the natural philosophy of the earliest human cultures, for it embodies a cosmology rooted in that most primal and wondrous presence: earth's mysterious generative force. Again we sense this is a worldview that survived outside the mythological power structure of the Shang theocracy, for it is a female-centered system quite the opposite of the male-centered Shang system. This generative force must have been truly wondrous to those primal people not only because of the unending miracle of new life seemingly appearing from nothing, but also because that miracle was so immediately vital to their well-being, directly providing them with food, water, clothing, shelter, and, of course, a future in their children. And this wonder is often invoked in the *I Ching*:

> *How vast and wondrous the heaven of origins! . . . How vast its illumination of ends and beginnings! (1)*

> *How perfect and wondrous the earth of origins! (2)*

> *How vast, how utterly vast it is: the meaning of succession following its proper seasons! (17)*

> *How vast, how utterly vast it is: the meaning of the generative following its proper seasons! (44)*

Taoist thought describes the Cosmos as an ever-changing generative whole, and the Taoist term for this generative ontological process is *Tao*, meaning "Way," from its original meaning "road" or "pathway": the generative ontological process conceived as a "path*Way*." The *Tao Te Ching* speaks of it in explicitly female terms: "mother," "mother of all beneath heaven," "nurturing mother," "dark female-enigma." The term also appears a number of times in the *I Ching*, where it is clearly the same generative principle, and the Cosmos that the Way describes is everywhere, beginning with the book's first utterance:

> *All origins penetrating everywhere, heaven is inexhaustible in bringing forth wild bounty.*

And the Presentation elaborating on that Statement continues to develop the idea, introducing the concept of the Way:

> *How vast and wondrous the heaven of origins! The ten thousand things all begin from it. It governs the sky—the movement of clouds, the coming of rain. It gives all the various things their distinct forms. How vast its illumination of ends and beginnings! . . .*

> *The Way of heaven is all change and transformation at the hinge of things, where the unfurling nature of each thing itself is perfected.*

> *It nurtures vast harmony in wholeness, and remains inexhaustible in bringing forth wild bounty.*

The *Tao Te Ching* describes the Way's most fundamental form as "return." It says "return is the movement of the Way," and:

> *the ten thousand things arise,*
> *and in them I watch the return:*
> *all things on and ever on*
> *each returning to its root.*

Return is also spoken of as essential in the *I Ching*, where there is a hexagram dedicated to it: "Return" (24). The elaborations on this hexagram say, "All return penetrating everywhere, things emerge and die back . . ." and:

> *In return itself, you can see the very heart-mind of all heaven and earth.*

The ten thousand things emerge from and then return to a root or source, from which they reappear in a new form. Although this source is not specifically described in the *I Ching*, later Taoist/Ch'an (Zen) Buddhist texts developed a number of terms for it, such as "Absence," "emptiness," and "dark-enigma." But this is not absence or emptiness in the sense of a realm somehow outside the empirical. Instead, it is an absence or emptiness of forms. Or in other words, it is the undifferentiated ontological whole: the formless tissue that shapes itself into one configuration of form, one array of the ten thousand things, then reshapes itself into another through the process of death, transformation, and rebirth.

This is nothing other than the dynamic interaction of heaven and earth, in which any moment in the ongoing process of change is an origin place. This cosmology of "Way" and "return" leads to a very primal experience of time, an experience embedded in the uninflected verbs of classical Chinese that simply register action, occurrence appearing of itself. Rather than the linear progression the Western tradition assumes to be a kind of metaphysical river flowing past, time becomes an all-encompassing generative present, a constant burgeoning forth that includes everything we think of as past and future.

Remarkably, this primal concept of time is enacted in the formal architecture of the *I Ching*: we experience it there in the fragmentary structure and discontinuous utterances that frustrate linear thinking; in the layers of elaboration within which the text continually circles back on itself rather than simply moves forward in the usual linear way; and in the divination system of reading, which is decidedly nonlinear, and has no beginning or end. However you approach the *I Ching*, it feels like you are inhabiting a level below the surface of appearance, a level where the forces driving change move. From the standpoint of literature, it is in a sense the most powerful Taoist text, for in a philosophical system centered around the generative source, the *I Ching* is a text that still feels messy with origins.

The goal of a Taoist sage is to dwell as an integral part of the Cosmos, of the ceaseless unfolding of change. This is always a challenge because in the texture of our routine experience, we feel radically separate from the Cosmos. Its processes seem to go on outside of our self-enclosed mental ("spirit") realm. Language and perception are always directed at something "out there." *I Ching* divination practice operates on the very primal assumption that we are an integral part of the Cosmos. And further, it allows us to locate ourselves in the organic unfolding of the generative whole. And so, it is a practice of reintegrating ourselves into the ontological tissue. This practice of harmonizing with the movement of the Cosmos evolved into more profound dimensions in Taoist and Ch'an Buddhist thought and practice. Indeed, the arts too were considered spiritual practices in this sense: poetry, painting, calligraphy. But the *I Ching* is where such wisdom practices began.

The *Tao Te Ching* and *Chuang Tzu* try to coax us out of our self-enclosed spirit-centers into a broader experience of identity that includes all of the Way. They do that through dark and mysterious poetry, paradoxical insights, and zany storytelling. Ch'an teaching continued and refined these strategies, and meditation practices added an immediate experiential dimension. In meditation, you can watch thoughts emerge from emptiness and return back to that emptiness. This leads first to the realization that you are separate from those thoughts, which we normally identify with self. A second realization is that consciousness is the Way, too. Known in ancient Chinese as "heart-mind" (心), for no distinction was made between heart and mind, consciousness is made of the same generative tissue following the movement of return: thoughts and emotions appearing out of emptiness and returning to their root in that same emptiness. And finally, as thought and emotion fall silent, comes the realization that the root experienced there in consciousness, that empty source, is the source shared by all of the ten thousand things. And so, the source of the empirical Cosmos can paradoxically be described as "heart-mind":

In return itself, you can see the very heart-mind of all heaven and earth.

The weave of identity and Cosmos found in the *I Ching* and early Taoist texts derives from such a primal level of culture that it shaped the classical Chinese language from the beginning. This is most prominent in the language's wide-open grammar. Prepositions and conjunctions are rarely used, leaving relationships among lines, phrases, ideas, and images unclear. The distinction between singular and plural is only rarely and indirectly made. Verbs are not uncommonly absent, and when present they have no tenses, so temporal location and sequence are vague. Rather than linear time, they register action as the steady burgeoning forth of the Way in its movement of return. And very often subjects and objects are absent, which creates the sense of individual identities blurred together into a shared space of consciousness. It is a grammar of mystery, in which meaning must be drawn out of all this empty grammatical space, as if you were drawing it out of a primal mystery of origins, out of the dark origins where human culture begins, where change itself and the *Book of Change* too begin. The result is an experience of consciousness as a much more open and penetrating phenomenon than Western thought and language allow. It is an experience of consciousness woven integrally into the Cosmos.

This magical potential inherent to classical Chinese was used to great effect in later Taoist and poetic texts, but it is no less alive throughout the *I Ching*. It is especially noteworthy in the first four graphs of chapter 1 ("Heaven"), the first utterance in Chinese written culture. It feels like a kind of ur-language, somewhere between hexagrams and a more normally expressive language:

元	亨	利	貞
birth/	flourish/	harvest/	completion/
origin	penetrate	bounty	inexhaustible

The meanings of the graphs are not entirely clear, nor is the grammar that organizes them, and one can really begin to decipher them only after reading further into the text to develop some context within which to understand their cryptic code. To complicate things, the term *heaven* appears before them, naming the hexagram, and it isn't clear if it is also meant to be part of the sentence. The graphs may be a list of the essential characteristics defining the four seasons. Hence, assuming *heaven* is part of the sentence:

Heaven is birth and flourish, harvest and completion.

But the graphs are usually given a more philosophical cast. For 元, the range of meanings might also include: *origin, generative impulse, great, awe-inspiring*; for 亨: *penetrate, develop, success, prevalence*; for 利: *bounty, fitness, profit, effective*; and for 貞: *inexhaustible, constancy, upright and true, righteous.*

The wide-open grammar only complicates things further. The graphs might be read one by one, as some kind of oracular pronouncement:

Origin. Penetrating. Bountiful. Inexhaustible.

Or, taking *heaven* to be part of the utterance, it could be a list of adjectives describing heaven:

Heaven is origin, penetrating, bountiful, and inexhaustible.

The graphs might be read as two separate phrases with two graphs each:

Origin penetrates everywhere, and its bounty is inexhaustible.

Or, again taking *heaven* to be part of the utterance:

Heaven is penetrating origins and inexhaustible bounty.

And finally, the four graphs might be read together:

All origins penetrating everywhere, heaven is inexhaustible in bringing forth wild bounty.

This texture of open possibility suffuses every dimension of the *I Ching*, and has allowed it to evolve dramatically over the ages. Meanings of words themselves, divisions of text into phrases and sentences (classical Chinese had no punctuation), syntax and interpretation of those phrases and sentences: these all evolved according to the predilections of influential readers and different ages. And however a reader resolves all of these issues, the text remains a discontinuous series of profoundly mysterious utterances, which opened it to seemingly endless interpretive schemes over the centuries. Hence the *I Ching* has itself been a case study in its primary principle: change.

Building on the language's grammar of mystery, the *I Ching* is nothing less than a dance with mystery. Its remarkable architecture is designed to embody and enact mystery, for it allows the book to be read in a number of different ways. As a poetic/philosophical text, it can be read like any other text, from beginning to end. However, even in this conventional reading, the book frustrates expectations of coherence. It is made up of fragmentary utterances, mysterious enough in and of themselves. And these fragments often feel quite disparate in nature: poetry alternates with philosophy, bare image with storytelling, social and political with private and spiritual, plainspoken and earnest with satire and humor. These fragments often repeat in new contexts and variations and reversals. In this, the *I Ching* engages us with that mystery by continuously proffering the promise of understanding and wisdom, but before that promise is fulfilled, the text always moves on to another possibility, another moment in the movement of change, thereby breaking up and undermining the first. And it is there, in that evanescence, that real poetry and insight lie.

Reading the book through its divination architecture only intensifies this experience, for rather than reading from beginning to end, each time you begin reading, you begin in a new place determined by "chance." And of course, the book's architecture invites another way to read the text, perhaps the most common in actual practice among contemporary readers: wandering the text by reading randomly chosen passages. In either of these methods—divination or random wandering—the text is ever-changing and never-ending, and it is a different text for everyone who reads it. A mystery of enigmatic and often contradictory sayings set within a bewildering architecture: this is a book that never lets you come to a still point where you feel that you have reached some stable understanding. Always frustrating the long interpretive tradition that tried to make the text comprehensible and useful, the book takes mystery itself as its most profound dimension.

In this, the book is enacting the fundamental nature of the Cosmos itself. Even after the most exhaustive and accurate scientific or philosophical account, the most compelling mythology, or the most concise and penetrating poem, the ten thousand things remain, in and of themselves, a mystery beyond us. In China, this mystery of things was seen from early times as a kind of silence, an absence of linguistic knowing, and it was considered the deepest wisdom. The hexagrams are as close as human inscription can come to that silence, and the *I Ching* text with its fleeting utterances also hews close to that silence. It sometimes suggests this directly, as in the Presentation for hexagram 47, for instance:

> When there's talk, there's no sincerity, no accuracy. *Revere words, and you soon wither impoverished away.*

This skepticism about language and understanding is fundamental in Taoist and Ch'an Buddhist thought, with their various strategies for seeing through the conventional structures of thought and identity. And so the *I Ching*'s architecture of mystery was no doubt its most profound appeal among more sober-minded intellectuals who were fundamentally shaped by Taoist and Ch'an Buddhist practices, the artists and writers who created ancient Chinese culture. In the seminal Taoist texts—*Tao Te Ching* and *Chuang Tzu*—they tangled with paradoxical utterances and ideas made more mysterious by fragmentary forms not unlike the *I Ching*'s. In Ch'an Buddhism they tangled with even more paradoxical texts, encountered the wild and surprising antics of sage teachers, gave themselves to meditation practice. All of these strategies were designed to tease the mind outside workaday assumptions and linguistic structures, outside the limitations of identity. In the *I Ching* we find similar literary strategies in more primeval forms; and this translation tries to emphasize this "literary *I Ching*," the one that would have most deeply engaged ancient intellectuals.

For those artists and monks and writers, the sage lives most authentically on the edge where language and identity weave into the ontological tissue of change as a whole. *Aren't we each another fleeting form in that tissue's process of perpetual transformation?* they might ask. *Isn't our fullest identity that tissue itself? Isn't it all and none of earth's fleeting forms simultaneously?* To read the *I Ching* like this, as mystery given evanescent shape in poetry and philosophy, is to return to the origin place where heaven and earth interact in that all-encompassing generative present, to our own primal origins, our place at the wellsprings of change. It is, in fact, to become dragon again.

I CHING

HEAVEN

All origins penetrating everywhere, heaven is inexhaustible in bringing forth wild bounty.

PRESENTATION

How vast and wondrous the heaven of origins! The ten thousand things all begin from it. It governs the sky—the movement of clouds, the coming of rain. It gives all the various things their distinct forms. How vast its illumination of ends and beginnings!

When the potent places of these six lines are realized in their proper seasons, the seasons mount the six sun-dragons and soar through the sky.

The Way of heaven is all change and transformation at the hinge of things, where the unfurling nature of each thing itself is perfected. It nurtures vast harmony in wholeness, and remains inexhaustible in bringing forth wild bounty. When its dragon-head rears up among the innumerable things, it unites the ten thousand kingdoms in wholeness and peace.

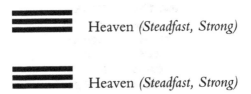 Heaven *(Steadfast, Strong)*

Heaven *(Steadfast, Strong)*

IMAGE
Heaven's movement is steadfast and strong. Using it, the noble-minded fortify themselves without cease.

LINES
I
The dragon rests, hidden underwater, and nothing happens.

2
The dragon appears in open fields. Seek advice from a great sage, and wild bounty will prevail.

3
For the noble-minded, it's heaven and heaven and heaven all day long. And at night, their awe at its transformations is like an affliction. How could they ever go astray?

4
Some may even leap into the abyss, and still not go astray.

5
The dragon soars in open sky. Seek advice from a great sage, and wild bounty will prevail.

6
The dragon grows high and mighty, and so comes to grief.

2

EARTH

All origins penetrating everywhere, earth is inexhaustible as a mare horse in bringing forth wild bounty. And so it is that when the noble-minded set out in the lead toward a destination, they soon fall into confusion; but when they follow, they reach the bounty of that wondrous host. Finding friends on southwest plains, losing friends in northeast mountains—the noble-minded remain inexhaustible and serene, and so come to good fortune.

PRESENTATION

How perfect and wondrous the earth of origins! The ten thousand things are all born from it. Yielding and devoted as a river, it supports the sky. It carries things along in its generosity, joins them boundlessly in its heart-sight clarity, opens them away all vast radiance in its embrace. And it unites all the various things in wholeness penetrating everywhere.

A mare horse is like the land, for it roams the land boundlessly.

All tender assent, yielding and devoted as a river, earth is inexhaustible in bringing forth wild bounty. *And so it is that when the noble-minded set out in the lead toward a destination, they soon fall into confusion* and lose the Way. But when they follow, yielding and devoted as a river, they master constancy. *Finding friends on southwest plains*, they move with kindred spirits. *Losing friends in northeast mountains*, they know blessings whole and through to completion. Inexhaustible and serene in their good fortune, they live boundless as the land.

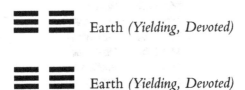 Earth *(Yielding, Devoted)*

Earth *(Yielding, Devoted)*

IMAGE

The land's power: that is *Earth*. Using it, the noble-minded carry things along with earth's generosity, its heart-sight clarity.

LINES
I
When there's frost underfoot, how perfectly ice will soon form!
2
In its own place vast, earth never struggles, and yet there is no bounty it does not bring forth.
3
Harbor beauty within, and you'll be inexhaustible indeed. If perhaps you undertake an emperor's business, don't scramble for quick results and there will be wholeness.
4
Wrap it all up together in a sack and hide yourself away. Though you'll earn no praise, how could you ever go astray?
5
Wear robes of yellow, color of the earth, and you dwell at the very origins of good fortune.
6
Dragons battle in the countryside, their blood black and yellow, colors of heaven and earth.

BIRTH-THROE

All origins penetrating everywhere, birth-throe is inexhaustible in bringing forth wild bounty. Still, nothing happening: that is where you set forth. Trusting sage-advisors brings forth wild bounty.

PRESENTATION

Birth-throe is tender assent just beginning to mingle with everything steely as a mountain in cloud. That means birth will be long, hard work.

In a moment of such danger, whatever stirs must be vast and inexhaustible in penetrating everywhere. When thunder and rain stir, for instance, they incite all fruition and abundance.

Heaven, that birth-chamber of things—it's everywhere dark chaos and confusion. There's no repose, even in trusting sage-advisors.

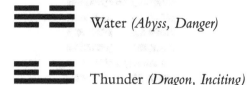 Water *(Abyss, Danger)*

Thunder *(Dragon, Inciting)*

IMAGE

Cloud and thunder: that is *Birth-Throe*. Using it, the noble-minded weave order from the loom of origins.

LINES

1

Struggle without progress. Dwelling in the inexhaustible brings forth wild bounty, and trusting sage-advisors too brings forth wild bounty.

2

Birth-throe: What is it like? It's like an impasse, like teams of horses pulling against each other. The man proposing marriage is hardly a tyrant, but the young girl is inexhaustible in refusing. Only after ten years does she agree to marry.

3

Hunting deer through deep forests without a guide, even the noble-minded are soon lost. Set out like that and your journey will be difficult indeed.

4

It's like teams of horses pulling against each other, like searching for a young girl to marry. Setting out brings good fortune, for there's wild bounty in whatever you do.

5

Birth-throe is fertile richness. If you're inexhaustible in small things, good fortune will prevail. If you're inexhaustible in great things, calamity can't be far away.

6

It's like teams of horses pulling against each other, like tears of blood flowing and flowing.

4

INCEPTION-THICKET

It's all inception-thicket penetrating everywhere. I don't seek out inception in its thicket of youth; inception seeks me out in its thicket of youth. If people inquire once with shaman-flower sticks, I answer. If they inquire again, it's deep confusion; and of deep confusion, I say nothing. There, the inception-thicket is inexhaustible in bringing forth wild bounty.

PRESENTATION

Inception is the dangerous thicket beneath mountains, and to stop in that dangerous thicket is also inception.

It's all inception-thicket penetrating everywhere. Use it and you move ahead, penetrating everywhere, centered always in your proper season.

I don't seek out inception in its thicket of youth; inception seeks me out in its thicket of youth. This is to share the same intention.

If people inquire once with shaman-flower sticks, I answer. This is to be centered as a steely mountain in cloud. *If they inquire again, it's deep confusion; and of deep confusion, I say nothing.* This deep confusion is the inception-thicket. And using this inception-thicket to foster the hinge of things: that is the mastery of a great sage.

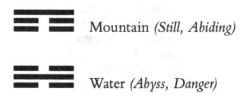 Mountain *(Still, Abiding)*

Water *(Abyss, Danger)*

IMAGE

A spring welling up beneath mountains: that is *Inception-Thicket.*
Using it, the noble-minded ponder every consequence of their actions;
and so, they foster heart-sight clarity.

LINES

I

Inception-thicket in its first stirrings: Use it to discipline people, and
you can bring forth wild bounty. Use it to liberate shackles and fetters,
and you can set out through difficult journeys.

2

Embrace the inception-thicket, and good fortune will prevail. Take a
wife, and good fortune follows. It is always a child who one day leads
the family.

3

Don't use the inception-thicket's first stirrings to choose a woman who
only sees men of gold. Don't cling to yourself, for there's wild bounty
in having no destination.

4

Inception-thicket in its exhaustion: A difficult journey.

5

Inception-thicket in its youth: Good fortune.

6

Inception-thicket in its violence: Tyranny and intimidation bring forth
no bounty. It is guarding against tyranny and intimidation that brings
forth wild bounty.

ANTICIPATION

In anticipation, nurture the dedication of a bird sitting on eggs.
Inexhaustible and penetrating radiant everywhere, it rains down good
fortune. Crossing a great river brings forth wild bounty.

PRESENTATION

Anticipation is waiting, is knowing danger lies ahead. Steadfast and
strong as a steely mountain in cloud, you won't get snared in lurking
danger. And so, you won't live in exhaustion withering
impoverished away.

*In anticipation, nurture the dedication of a bird sitting on eggs. Inexhaustible and
penetrating radiant everywhere, it rains down good fortune.* Dwell where
heaven's potent place is your own potent place, and you dwell centered
at the hinge of things.

Crossing a great river brings forth wild bounty. Setting out is where great
achievement begins.

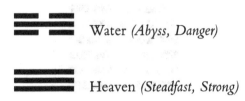

Water *(Abyss, Danger)*

Heaven *(Steadfast, Strong)*

IMAGE

Clouds rising into the sky before rain: that is *Anticipation*. Using it, the noble-minded find stillness and joy in simply eating and drinking.

LINES

I

Anticipation among farmland fertility altars: If you rely on moondrift constancy to bring forth great bounty, how could you ever go astray?

2

Anticipation on the river's sandy shores: Even if there is a little small-minded worry and talk, good fortune will endure whole and through to completion.

3

Anticipation mired in mud: You'll be set upon by thieves.

4

Anticipation mired in blood: You must leave home.

5

Anticipation with food and wine: Good fortune will be inexhaustible.

6

Returning home you find guests have arrived, three uninvited guests. Honor them, and good fortune will endure whole and through to completion.

DISCORD

In discord, nurture the dedication of a bird sitting on eggs. Facing constraints, settle in and look upon them with awe, then you'll be centered in good fortune. Force through constraints to the end, and you'll know calamity. Seeking advice from a great sage brings forth wild bounty. Crossing a great river brings forth no bounty.

PRESENTATION

Discord is danger below a steely mountain in cloud. To be steadfast and strong in the face of danger: that is this same discord.

In discord, nurture the dedication of a bird sitting on eggs. Facing constraints, settle in and look upon them with awe, then you'll be centered in good fortune. Facing constraints like this means you arrive steely as a mountain in cloud and settle in at the abiding center of things.

Force through constraints to the end, and you'll know calamity. Forcing through like this means discord cannot come to completion.

Seeking advice from a great sage brings forth wild bounty. Seeking advice like this means you revere life centered at the hinge of things.

Crossing a great river brings forth no bounty. Crossing like this means you fall into an abyss.

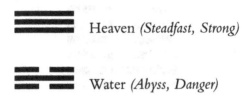 Heaven *(Steadfast, Strong)*

Water *(Abyss, Danger)*

IMAGE

Heaven and water seething in opposition: that is *Discord*. Using it, the noble-minded plan the first steps in their endeavors.

LINES

I

Don't drag your endeavors out on and on. Even if there is a little small-minded worry and talk, good fortune will endure whole and through to completion.

2

If you can't master discord, leave town and go back home. Then the townspeople will be without injury, all three hundred households.

3

Nourished by ancient heart-sight clarity, inexhaustible through affliction: this brings good fortune whole and through to completion. If perhaps you undertake an emperor's business, don't scramble for quick results.

4

If you can't master discord, return to the inevitable unfurling of things in their transformations. There you will be inexhaustible and serene, and so come to good fortune.

5

Discord is the very origin of good fortune.

6

If perhaps a sash of honor is bestowed upon you some morning, it will be stripped away three times before morning ends.

7

ARMIES

When armies are inexhaustible and sage-elders lead them, good fortune prevails and nothing goes astray.

PRESENTATION

Armies are the people in multitudes, are inexhaustible at the hinge of things. A sage-elder who can marshal multitudes at the hinge of things is worthy of being emperor. If he is centered like a steely mountain in cloud, those multitudes are centered and steely. When he leads them through danger, they are yielding and devoted as a river. A sage-elder like this nourishes all beneath heaven, so the people follow. And with such good fortune, how could anything go astray?

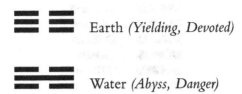

Earth *(Yielding, Devoted)*

Water *(Abyss, Danger)*

IMAGE

Water under the earth, sustaining it: that is *Armies*. Using them, the noble-minded husband the people and nurture multitudes.

LINES

I

When armies set out, they do so according to laws. Without laws, calamity prevails.

2

At the center of armies, a sage-elder brings forth good fortune and never goes astray. The emperor issues commendations of praise again and again and again.

3

When armies start stacking corpses on war carts, calamity has come.

4

If armies retreat to a safe place, it doesn't mean they've gone astray.

5

If there is game in the fields, hunting brings forth wild bounty and nothing goes astray. But if an elder child leads armies, the younger child stacks corpses on war carts. Calamity like that is inexhaustible indeed.

6

Great rulers inhabit the inevitable unfurling of things. They open kingdoms and nourish families. The small-minded aren't capable of such things.

CONFLUENCE

Confluence means good fortune, means inquiring at the source with shaman-flower sticks, where you live all origins inexhaustible on and on. How could you ever go astray? People from lands in turmoil will come flocking to you, knowing that whoever waits will meet with calamity.

PRESENTATION

Confluence is good fortune. Confluence is support, is following along humbly, yielding and devoted as a river.

Inquiring at the source with shaman-flower sticks, where you live all origins inexhaustible on and on. How could you ever go astray? In this, you live centered as a steely mountain in cloud.

People from lands in turmoil will come flocking to you, and both lofty and lowly will concur in you.

Whoever waits will meet with calamity, for their Way is soon exhausted and lost.

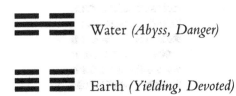

Water *(Abyss, Danger)*

Earth *(Yielding, Devoted)*

IMAGE

Water on the earth, flowing always together: that is *Confluence.* Using it, the first emperors founded the ten thousand kingdoms and made a family of all the lords and princes in those kingdoms.

LINES

1

Begin in confluence, with the dedication of a bird sitting on eggs, and you never go astray. Live as a vessel brimful, with the dedication of a bird sitting on eggs, and you live at ease with good fortune whole and through to completion.

2

Begin in confluence growing from all that lies within you, and good fortune is inexhaustible indeed.

3

Confluence begins with strangers.

4

When everything beyond is where confluence begins, good fortune is inexhaustible indeed.

5

The bright manifestation of confluence is like the emperor's hunt: animals are chased toward him on both sides and behind, while they scatter free in front. When the townspeople need no commands, good fortune prevails.

6

When confluence begins without the Way, calamity prevails.

DELICATE NURTURING

Delicate nurturing penetrates everywhere. Laden clouds bring no rain. They drift away past our fertility altars in the west.

PRESENTATION

Delicate nurturing. When tender assent occupies its potent place, when lofty and lowly concur in it: that is called *delicate nurturing*.

Steadfast and strong, reverent and inward, centered as a steely mountain in cloud, you realize your ambition, letting it penetrate everywhere.

Laden clouds bring no rain. Set out like this in reverence. *They drift away past our fertility altars in the west.* It's always true your influence may fail to spread.

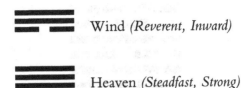

Wind *(Reverent, Inward)*

Heaven *(Steadfast, Strong)*

IMAGE

Wind spreading above heaven: that is *Delicate Nurturing.* Using it, the noble-minded refine heart-sight clarity's elegance in the grain of things.

LINES

1

Begin your return in the Way itself, and you never go astray. You'll know good fortune instead.

2

Even if you are herded along through that return, you'll know good fortune.

3

Forcing ahead until they shatter spokes from their cartwheels, husband and wife glare at each other.

4

When you possess the dedication of a bird sitting on eggs, blood eases away and awe emerges. And then, you never go astray.

5

When you possess the dedication of a bird sitting on eggs, when it binds you with neighbors like silk thread and work and words, everyone is enriched.

6

If there's rain, there's a dwelling-place. Make the reverence of heart-sight clarity your starting point. For a woman, affliction is inexhaustible. If the noble-minded wait through full moon after full moon before forging ahead, calamity can't be far away.

WALKING

Walk on a tiger's tail without being eaten, and you penetrate everywhere.

PRESENTATION

To walk with tender assent is to walk steely as a mountain in cloud, your delight concurring with heaven. Walking like that, you *walk on a tiger's tail without being eaten, and you penetrate everywhere.*

Centered as a steely mountain in cloud, you move at the hinge of things. Walking in that potent place of sovereignty, there's no flaw anywhere. Instead, it's all radiant illumination.

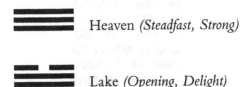

Heaven *(Steadfast, Strong)*

Lake *(Opening, Delight)*

IMAGE

Heaven above and lake below: that is *Walking*. Using it, the noble-minded differentiate above and below, lofty and lowly. That's how they ground the purpose of the people.

LINES

1

Set out walking with the simplicity of origin's weave, and you never go astray.

2

Walking a path level and smooth, deep with contentment, a recluse living in dark mystery is inexhaustible in good fortune.

3

One eye gone, you can still see. One leg lame, you can still walk. But if you can't walk on a tiger's tail without being eaten, calamity can't be far away. That's how it is for a warrior who imagines himself a great ruler.

4

Walk on a tiger's tail in fear and circumspect awe, and good fortune will prevail whole and through to completion.

5

Walk with resolute certainty, and you walk inexhaustible through affliction.

6

If you can still see and still walk, you can test the limits of all these blessings, of how things always return to the very origins of good fortune.

DEVOTION

In small devotion, you set out. In vast devotion, you arrive. And so, good fortune penetrates everywhere.

PRESENTATION

In small devotion, you set out. In vast devotion, you arrive. And so, good fortune penetrates everywhere. In devotion, heaven and earth weave together, earth settling into heaven's rising, and so the ten thousand things open through one another. Lofty and lowly weave together, and so they share the same purpose.

In devotion, *yang* abides within, *yin* without. Steadfast and strong abide within, yielding and devoted without. The noble-minded abide within, the small-minded without.

The Way endures in the noble-minded, bleeds away in the small-minded.

▦▦ Earth *(Yielding, Devoted)*

▬▬ Heaven *(Steadfast, Strong)*

IMAGE

Heaven and earth weaving together, earth settling into heaven's rising:
that is *Devotion*. Using it, Mother-Empress enriches and completes the
Way of heaven and earth. And to support the accord of heaven and
earth, she uses the people tending fields in every direction.

LINES

1

We harvest thatch-grass whole, roots and all. And so, much more
comes with it. Forge ahead in this way and good fortune will prevail.

2

Embrace the boundless wilds and cross the river. Never let those
distances go. Then, even with friends disappearing, you will move
reverent at the abiding center of things.

3

Without valley there is no mountain. Without leaving there is no
return. And if you are inexhaustible in the face of difficulties, how
could you ever go astray? Nurture the dedication of a bird sitting on
eggs. Never doubt it. Then a simple meal will feel like such a blessing.

4

Wings, their delicate feathers, flutter and flutter. Never use neighbors
to enrich yourself. Never use the dedication of a bird sitting on eggs to
shield yourself.

5

When a girl comes home in marriage to Lord Burgeon, blessings arise
at the origins of good fortune.

6

When city walls crumble, returning to the bastion-trench outside, don't
call up armies. Limit your commands to the city itself. The difficulties
of your journey will be inexhaustible indeed.

OBSTRUCTION

When the noble-minded face obstruction by malevolent people, even their most inexhaustible efforts bring forth no bounty. Therefore, a great sage leaves when the small-minded arrive.

PRESENTATION

When the noble-minded face obstruction by malevolent people, even their most inexhaustible efforts bring forth no bounty. Therefore, a great sage leaves when the small-minded arrive. In obstruction, the weave of heaven and earth unravels, earth settling away from heaven's rising, and so the ten thousand things no longer open through one another. The weave of lofty and lowly unravels, and so all beneath heaven becomes a confusion of crumbling nations.

In obstruction, *yin* abides within, *yang* without. Tender assent abides within, steely as a mountain in cloud without. The small-minded abide within, the noble-minded without.

The Way endures in the small-minded, bleeds away in the noble-minded.

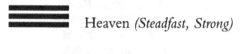 Heaven *(Steadfast, Strong)*

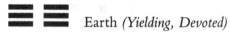 Earth *(Yielding, Devoted)*

IMAGE

The weave of heaven and earth unraveled, earth settling away from heaven's rising: that is *Obstruction*. Using it, the noble-minded guard heart-sight clarity and elude danger, so how could they accept offers of wealth and renown?

LINES

1

We harvest thatch-grass whole, roots and all. And so, much more comes with it. In this way, inexhaustible good fortune penetrates everywhere.

2

Struggling for reward, the small-minded find good fortune. But for a great sage, obstruction penetrates everywhere.

3

In such struggles, there is only shame.

4

Inhabit the inevitable unfurling of things, and you never go astray. This is how you bring blessings to people near and far.

5

At rest in obstruction, a great sage finds good fortune. Is he lost, is he lost? He's tethered always to the mulberry burgeoning from seed.

6

Obstruction always crumbles apart in the end. First comes obstruction, then joy.

13

KINDRED SPIRITS

Together in wildlands, kindred spirits penetrate everywhere. Crossing a great river brings forth wild bounty. And in bringing forth wild bounty, the noble-minded are inexhaustible.

PRESENTATION

In tender assent, kindred spirits find a potent place, find an abiding center, and so concur with heaven.

Together in wildlands, kindred spirits penetrate everywhere. Crossing a great river brings forth wild bounty. This is the movement of heaven.

Steadfast and strong inhabiting that illumination in the grain of things, centered at the hinge of things and concurring with heaven: for the noble-minded, that is the hinge of things.

Those who open through the purpose of all beneath heaven: they are the noble-minded.

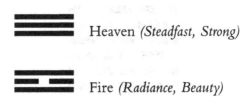

Heaven *(Steadfast, Strong)*

Fire *(Radiance, Beauty)*

IMAGE
Heaven and fire: that is *Kindred Spirits*. Using it, the noble-minded rely on how things are the same to see how things differ.

LINES
1
Together at the gate, kindred spirits never go astray.
2
Together at the ancestral source, kindred spirits find the journey ahead difficult indeed.
3
You may prevail by hiding armies in thick forests or leading them across high ridgelines, but even after waiting three years you should never use them.
4
If you conquer the city wall, but don't subdue the people, good fortune will prevail.
5
Among kindred spirits, tears come first, then laughter. Only by gathering together in great armies can the people subdue an enemy.
6
Together at farmland fertility altars, kindred spirits live free of regret.

VAST PRESENCE
Vast Presence penetrates all origins everywhere.

PRESENTATION
All tender assent, vast Presence occupies a potent and venerable place, a vast and abiding center where lofty and lowly move always in concurrence.

Heart-sight clarity steadfast and strong, steely as a mountain in cloud, it inhabits that illumination in the grain of things.

Concurring with heaven, moving according to its proper seasons: that's how it *penetrates all origins everywhere.*

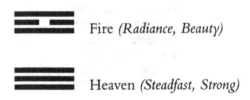

Fire *(Radiance, Beauty)*

Heaven *(Steadfast, Strong)*

IMAGE

Fire blazing above heaven: that is *Vast Presence*. Using it, the noble-minded prevent everything broken and evil, and they promote everything whole and good. Yielding and devoted as a river, heaven rests in the inevitable unfurling of things.

LINES

1

If you never let yourself get tangled in destructive ways, you never go astray. Even in difficulty, you never go astray.

2

With vast carts for transport, and Presence as your point of departure, you never go astray.

3

A true duke penetrates everywhere offering vast Presence to the emperor. Small-minded people can't manage this.

4

Even without strength and plenty, you never go astray.

5

When the dedication of a bird sitting on eggs weaves us together, when it makes a majestic people of us, good fortune prevails.

6

When it's from heaven that blessings emerge, good fortune prevails, never failing to bring forth wild bounty.

HUMILITY

All humility penetrating everywhere, as if bundling cut grain into sheaves, the noble-minded live whole and through to completion.

PRESENTATION

All humility penetrating everywhere, as if bundling cut grain into sheaves, heaven in its Way descends to nurture things with radiant illumination. And earth in its Way ascends from low and unnoticed beginnings.

It's the Way of heaven to reduce excess and augment humility, the Way of earth to transform excess and spread humility. It's the Way of ghosts and spirits to ravage excess and enrich humility, the Way of people to despise excess and love humility.

When Humility is lofty and revered, it is radiant; when it's low and unnoticed, there's no violating it. This is how the noble-minded live whole and through to completion.

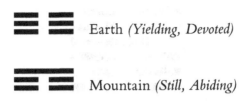

Earth *(Yielding, Devoted)*

Mountain *(Still, Abiding)*

IMAGE

Mountains at the earth's abiding center: that is *Humility*. Using it, the noble-minded deplete plenty and augment paucity, and so share things out everywhere equally.

LINES

1

Embracing humility, all humility penetrating everywhere, as if bundling cut grain into sheaves, the noble-minded cross a great river, and so bring forth good fortune.

2

Hear birdsong in humility, as if bundling cut grain into sheaves, and good fortune will be inexhaustible indeed.

3

Working diligently at humility, as if bundling cut grain into sheaves, the noble-minded bring forth good fortune whole and through to completion.

4

Fluttering banners of humility, as if bundling cut grain into sheaves, how can you fail to bring forth wild bounty?

5

Never using neighbors to enrich yourself, finding bounty even when setting out, how can you fail to bring forth wild bounty?

6

Hear birdsong in humility, as if bundling cut grain into sheaves, and you'll find wild bounty even when sending the people in armies to attack cities and kingdoms.

CONTENTMENT

In contentment, you depend on sage-advisors when sending the people to war in armies, and so bring forth wild bounty.

PRESENTATION

In contentment, you concur with everything steely as a mountain in cloud, and so bring your purpose to completion.

Yielding and devoted as a river in your actions, you live in contentment. Heaven and earth are full of this same contentment, always yielding and devoted as a river in their actions, so how could you fail to depend on sage-advisors when sending the people to war in armies?

Because heaven and earth are always yielding and devoted as a river in their actions, sun and moon never falter and the four seasons never waver.

A sage ruler is yielding and devoted as a river in his actions. He keeps crimes and punishments perfectly clear, and so the people submit willingly.

How vast, how utterly vast it is: the meaning of contentment following its proper seasons!

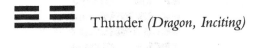 Thunder *(Dragon, Inciting)*

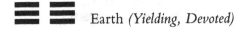 Earth *(Yielding, Devoted)*

IMAGE

At earth's appearance, thunder opening out: that is *Contentment*. Using it, the first emperors made music in veneration to heart-sight clarity, offered it in ravishing sacrifice to their Celestial Lord, and so made themselves worthy of their ancestors.

LINES

1

Hear birdsong in contentment, even knowing calamity can't be far away.

2

If you're hard as stone, never living days whole and through to completion, good fortune will be inexhaustible indeed.

3

Eyes bright with the arrogance of contentment, you come to regret. Progress slow with the hesitation of contentment, you come to regret.

4

Out of contentment comes vast Presence. Have no suspicions, and you will gather friends as a hairpin gathers hair.

5

Even through inexhaustible sickness and longing, moondrift constancy never dies.

6

When the shadowy mystery of contentment is complete, it still keeps changing, so how could it ever go astray?

SUCCESSION

All origins penetrating everywhere, succession is inexhaustible in bringing forth wild bounty. In succession, nothing goes astray.

PRESENTATION

Succession is everything steely as a mountain in cloud, arriving and dwelling all tender assent in humility. It moves with the dragon's inciting force all opening and delight.

Vast and inexhaustible in penetrating everywhere, succession never goes astray. And so all beneath heaven follows succession in its proper seasons.

How vast, how utterly vast it is: the meaning of succession following its proper seasons!

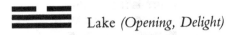 Lake *(Opening, Delight)*

Thunder *(Dragon, Inciting)*

IMAGE

Thunder at the lake's abiding center: that is *Succession*. Using it,
the noble-minded return home at nightfall to find sustenance and ease.

LINES

1

If you inhabit change, your good fortune will be inexhaustible indeed.
And setting out from your gate, mingling in the world, you will
accomplish great things.

2

Hold fast to the child, and you lose the sage-elder.

3

Hold fast to the sage-elder, and you lose the child. Through succession
you find whatever you seek, and so live in wild and inexhaustible
bounty.

4

Through succession you find rewards, but also inexhaustible calamity.
Through the Way of succession, you find the dedication of a bird sitting
on eggs. You find deep illumination. How could you ever go astray?

5

Infuse your nobility with the dedication of a bird sitting on eggs, and
good fortune will prevail.

6

Hold fast to things and move with them. Moored to things like this,
moving with them, Emperor T'ai penetrated everywhere through to
Bowhand Mountain.

MAGGOT-BOWL

All origins penetrating everywhere, decay's maggot-bowl brings forth the wild bounty of crossing a great river. Before every turning point, there are three transition days. After every turning point, there are three transition days.

PRESENTATION

Decay's maggot-bowl is steely as a mountain in cloud above, all tender assent below. Reverent and inward, still and abiding: that is decay's maggot-bowl.

All origins penetrating everywhere, decay's maggot-bowl gives order to all beneath heaven.

The wild bounty of crossing a great river. That is to set out on your life's work.

Before every turning point, there are three transition days. After every turning point, there are three transition days. In every end is a beginning. This is the movement of heaven.

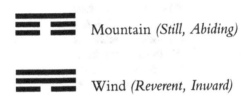

Mountain *(Still, Abiding)*

Wind *(Reverent, Inward)*

IMAGE

Beneath mountains, wind blowing: that is *Maggot-Bowl*. Using it, the noble-minded stir the people into action and foster heart-sight clarity.

LINES

I

Decay's maggot-bowl governs a father, and from that comes a child. And so, even when the father dies, nothing goes astray. From affliction comes good fortune whole and through to completion.

2

Decay's maggot-bowl governs a mother, so how inexhaustible can she be?

3

Decay's maggot-bowl governs a father, and from that comes little regret, for nothing vast goes astray.

4

Decay's maggot-bowl enriches a father, and from that beginning you can see a difficult journey.

5

Decay's maggot-bowl governs a father, and from that comes high praise.

6

Avoid serving emperors or their sage-advisors, then your life's work will ascend to lofty heights.

19

LONG VIEW

All origins penetrating everywhere, the long view is inexhaustible in bringing forth wild bounty. Even so, the eighth month inevitably brings calamity.

PRESENTATION

Mastering the long view, you become steely as a mountain in cloud and grow wise by brimming gradually out into flood, all opening and delight, yielding and devoted as a river. Steely as a mountain in cloud, you move at the abiding center of things, move always in concurrence with things.

Vast in penetrating everywhere, you abide at the hinge of things. That is the Way of heaven.

The eighth month inevitably brings calamity. The ravages of age are never long in coming.

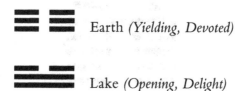 Earth *(Yielding, Devoted)*

Lake *(Opening, Delight)*

IMAGE
Above a lake, earth opening out: that is *Long View.* Using it, the noble-minded teach tirelessly, boundless in their care for the people.

LINES
1
See the long view whole, and good fortune is inexhaustible indeed.
2
See the long view whole, and good fortune never fails to bring forth wild bounty.
3
Sweeten the long view, and there's wild bounty in having no destination. Worry over it, and you never go astray.
4
Inhabit the long view, and you never go astray.
5
Understand the long view, and you live in accord with the great rulers. Then good fortune prevails.
6
Teach the long view, and good fortune prevails. How could you ever go astray?

HERON'S-EYE GAZE

As if purified in preparation for a sacrifice never offered: heron's-eye gaze is like that. It's like majesty infusing the dedication of a bird sitting on eggs.

PRESENTATION

This vast heron's-eye gaze is noble and lofty. It's reverent and inward, yielding and devoted as a river.

Centered at the hinge of things, you see all beneath heaven with this heron's-eye gaze.

As if purified in preparation for a sacrifice never offered: heron's-eye gaze is like that. It's like majesty infusing the dedication of a bird sitting on eggs. Seeing things with that heron's-eye gaze, the humble and lowly are transformed.

See heaven's spirit Way with that heron's-eye gaze, and it's clear the four seasons never waver. A great sage makes that spirit Way the foundation of his teaching, and so all beneath heaven pledges loyalty to him.

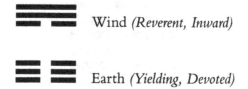 Wind *(Reverent, Inward)*

Earth *(Yielding, Devoted)*

IMAGE

Wind sweeping across the earth: that is *Heron's-Eye Gaze*. Using it, the first emperors traveled their lands gazing into the lives of the people, and they made that the foundation of their teaching.

LINES

1

Possessing the heron's-eye gaze of a child, the small-minded never go astray. But for the noble-minded, it's a difficult journey indeed.

2

Her gaze deep as this heron's eye through a gate, a woman is inexhaustible in bringing forth wild bounty.

3

Seeing our lives with this heron's-eye gaze, you see advances and setbacks.

4

See the nation's radiance with this heron's-eye gaze, consider it the emperor's guest, and great bounty will prevail.

5

Seeing our lives with this heron's-eye gaze, the noble-minded never go astray.

6

Seeing their own lives with this heron's-eye gaze, the noble-minded never go astray.

BITING FORESIGHT

Bring people together through the biting foresight of shaman-flower sticks, and you'll penetrate everywhere. Exact the proper punishments, and you'll bring forth wild bounty.

PRESENTATION

Something blocking the jaws of it all: that is when we say *bring people together through the biting foresight of shaman-flower sticks*. Bring people together through the biting foresight of shaman-flower sticks, then you'll penetrate everywhere.

Tender assent, steely as a mountain in cloud: when they are split apart by the dragon's inciting force, there is illumination. Lightning and thunder: when they join together, there is revelation.

Act from the abiding center of things, with tender assent, and your journey will be an ascent.

Exact the proper punishments, even when not in a potent place, and you'll bring forth wild bounty.

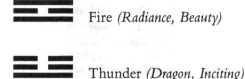

Fire *(Radiance, Beauty)*

Thunder *(Dragon, Inciting)*

IMAGE
Lightning and thunder: that is *Biting Foresight.* Using it, the first emperors illuminated punishments and perfected laws.

LINES
I
Shackle feet in punishment, even lop them off. How could you go astray?
2
If you can bite through fresh meat and lop off noses in punishment, all with the foresight of shaman-flower sticks, how could you go astray?
3
If you can bite through dried meat with the foresight of shaman-flower sticks, even if tasting poison, you'll never go astray and rarely even know difficulty in your journey.
4
If you can bite through heaven's bone and gristle with the foresight of shaman-flower sticks, bite through to the metal arrowhead, you'll find wild bounty in life's difficulties, and good fortune will be inexhaustible indeed.
5
If you can bite through heaven's meat with the foresight of shaman-flower sticks, bite through to the yellow metal of earth, you'll be inexhaustible through affliction. How could you ever go astray?
6
If you shackle necks in punishment and lop off ears, calamity will prevail.

ELEGANCE

Moving with the beauty of cowrie shells, elegance penetrates everywhere. And so, setting out toward a destination brings forth very little bounty.

PRESENTATION

Elegance penetrates everywhere. Coming all tender assent moving with the beauty of cowrie shells, you come steely as a mountain in cloud moving deep into the grain of things: and so, you penetrate everywhere.

Rising steely as a mountain in cloud moving with the beauty of cowrie shells, you rise all tender assent moving deep into the grain of things: and so, *setting out toward a destination brings forth very little bounty.*

It's the deep grain of heaven. To illuminate heaven's deep grain and abide there, that is the deep grain of people.

If you can see into the deep grain of heaven with a heron's-eye gaze, you can fathom the seasons and their transformations. If you can see into the deep grain of humankind with a heron's-eye gaze, you can transform and perfect all beneath heaven.

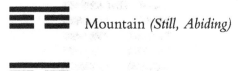 Mountain *(Still, Abiding)*

Fire *(Radiance, Beauty)*

IMAGE

Beneath mountains, fire: that is *Elegance*. Using it, the noble-minded illuminate the many dimensions of governing, for they know there's more to governing than settling court cases.

LINES

I

What elegance in her feet, as she steps down from the carriage and sets out among adepts walking!

2

What elegance in her downy cheek!

3

In such elegance, such glistening, good fortune is inexhaustible, is indeed unending.

4

In such elegance, such simplicity, she soars like the pellucid horse-star through the heavens. Never a thief marry.

5

What elegance in hills and gardens! Unfurled sheets of silk seem cheap and tawdry in comparison. Your journey will be difficult indeed, but it will bring good fortune whole and through to completion.

6

In pellucid elegance moving with the beauty of cowrie shells, you never go astray.

23

STRIPPING AWAY

Stripping away is setting out toward a destination that brings forth no bounty.

PRESENTATION

Stripping away is stripping away utterly, is tender assent transforming everything steely as a mountain in cloud.

Setting out toward a destination that brings forth no bounty. The small-minded are those who persist in this.

Still and abiding, yielding and devoted as a river: look into the image with a heron's-eye gaze.

The noble-minded revere ebb and flow, empty and full, for that is the movement of heaven.

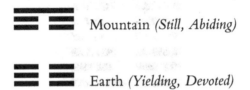

Mountain *(Still, Abiding)*

Earth *(Yielding, Devoted)*

IMAGE

Mountain clinging to earth: that is *Stripping Away.* Using it, the lofty
enrich the lowly, and so everyone dwells in peace.

LINES

1

Strip away the foot of their resting place, and destruction with its
inexhaustible calamity can't be far away.

2

Strip away the explanation of their resting place, and destruction with
its inexhaustible calamity can't be far away.

3

Strip it all away, and nothing goes astray.

4

Strip away the skin of their resting place, and calamity can't be far away.

5

String fish together with a temple priest's care, with a dragon's house-
hold kindness: How could that fail to bring forth wild bounty?

6

Ripe fruit still uneaten. The noble-minded offer their carriages, but the
small-minded strip even thatch huts away from the poor.

RETURN

All return penetrating everywhere, things emerge and die back without any anxious longing. Friends come without going astray. They turn back, returning to travel their own Way, and after seven days come, returning again. Setting out toward a destination brings forth wild bounty indeed.

PRESENTATION

All return penetrating everywhere, everything steely as a mountain in cloud turns back, moves with the dragon's inciting force, yielding and devoted as a river. This is to *emerge and die back without any anxious longing.*

Friends come without going astray. They turn back, returning to travel their own Way, and after seven days come, returning again. This is the movement of heaven.

Setting out toward a destination brings forth wild bounty indeed. In this, everything steely as a mountain in cloud persists.

In return itself, you can see the very heart-mind of all heaven and earth.

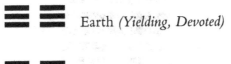 Earth *(Yielding, Devoted)*

Thunder *(Dragon, Inciting)*

IMAGE

Thunder at the earth's abiding center: that is *Return*. Using it, the first emperors closed borderland gates at the winter solstice. Merchants and travelers stayed home from their journeys, and lords stayed home from the inspection of their lands.

LINES

I

To return before going far, to be unconcerned with regret, that is to abide at the very origins of good fortune.

2

Rest in return, and good fortune will prevail.

3

Return is perennial. Even in affliction, nothing goes astray.

4

Moving at the abiding center of things, you return alone.

5

In the simplicity of return, there is no regret.

6

Tangle return in confusion, and calamity can't be far away. Answering disaster by sending the people to war in armies: that brings defeat and ruin whole and through to completion, utter calamity for a nation's rulers. Then, for ten years and more, they're too weak to forge anywhere ahead.

25

WISE-WOMAN INNOCENCE

All origins penetrating everywhere, wise-woman innocence is inexhaustible in bringing forth wild bounty. Abide in it at the hinge of things, or you'll meet trouble. Setting out toward a destination brings forth no bounty.

PRESENTATION

In wise-woman innocence, everything steely as a mountain in cloud comes from outside to become master of inside.

Infused with the dragon's inciting force, steadfast and strong, wise-woman innocence moves at the abiding center of things, moves steely as a mountain in cloud and always in concurrence with things.

To abide at the hinge of things, vast and penetrating everywhere, that is to inhabit the inevitable unfurling of heaven.

Abide in it at the hinge of things, or you'll meet trouble. Setting out toward a destination brings forth no bounty. If wise-woman innocence sets out, where is it going? And if it deserts the unfurling of heaven, what can it accomplish?

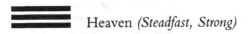 Heaven *(Steadfast, Strong)*

Thunder *(Dragon, Inciting)*

IMAGE

Thunder stirring throughout all beneath heaven: that is all things in
Wise-Woman Innocence. Using it, the first emperors thrived in accord
with the seasons and fostered the ten thousand things.

LINES

1

Set out with wise-woman innocence, and good fortune will come.

2

Harvest without plowing? Till without clearing land? Setting out
toward a destination brings forth wild bounty indeed.

3

Wise-woman innocence can bring disaster: an ox tethered and left
alone, for instance. It's a disaster for the villager, a boon for the vagabond.

4

If you're inexhaustible, you never go astray.

5

Wise-woman innocence can bring disease, but joy will come even
without medicine.

6

Even if you move with wise-woman innocence, you'll meet trouble.
There's wild bounty in having no destination.

VAST NURTURING

Vast nurturing is inexhaustible in bringing forth wild bounty. When those without a home are fed, good fortune prevails. Crossing a great river brings forth wild bounty.

PRESENTATION

Vast nurturing moves steadfast and strong and steely as a mountain in cloud, moves all bright radiance and true to the actual. Practice it, and you can renew heart-sight clarity day by day.

Attaining heights, steely as a mountain in cloud, you revere sage-elders.

If you abide in stillness steadfast and strong, you inhabit the great hinge of things.

When those without a home are fed, good fortune prevails. In this, you foster the wisdom of sage-elders.

Crossing a great river brings forth wild bounty. In this, you concur with heaven.

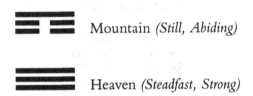

Mountain *(Still, Abiding)*

Heaven *(Steadfast, Strong)*

IMAGE

Heaven at the mountain's abiding center: that is *Vast Nurturing.* Using it, the noble-minded fathom the words and events of ancient times, and thereby nurture their heart-sight clarity.

LINES

1

Affliction too is wild bounty.

2

The cart has broken free of its axle.

3

To be inexhaustible through difficulty, like a fine horse in pursuit, brings forth wild bounty. People speak of a barrier-cart defense, but setting out toward a destination brings forth wild bounty indeed.

4

Wooden caps over the sharp horns of wild young bulls: such are the origins of good fortune.

5

Extract the boar's tusk and good fortune will prevail.

6

How is it the road of heaven penetrates everywhere?

JAWS OF IT ALL

In the jaws of it all, good fortune is inexhaustible indeed. Looking into the jaws of it all with that heron's-eye gaze, we each hunt out food to fill our bellies.

PRESENTATION

In the jaws of it all, good fortune is inexhaustible indeed. It's fostering the hinge of things that brings forth good fortune.

Looking into the jaws of it all with that heron's-eye gaze. This is the heron's-eye gaze into whatever fosters you.

We each hunt out food to fill our bellies. This is the heron's-eye gaze into whatever fosters you.

Like heaven and earth fostering the ten thousand things, a great sage fosters wise elders and thereby brings wisdom to the ten thousand people.

How vast, how utterly vast it is: the jaws of it all following their proper seasons!

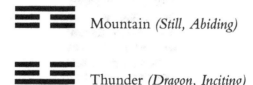

Mountain *(Still, Abiding)*

Thunder *(Dragon, Inciting)*

IMAGE

Beneath mountains, thunder: that is the *Jaws of It All.* Using it, the noble-minded instill their words and voices with caution, their food and drink with simplicity.

LINES

1

If you abandon divine oracle-bones for that heron's-eye gaze at our lives in the dangling jaws of it all, calamity will prevail.

2

Throw over the jaws of it all. Sweep its enduring loom-threads away into the hills. Once the jaws of it all sets forth, calamity has come.

3

Sweep the jaws of it all away, and calamity will continue inexhaustible indeed. Only after ten years will there be wild bounty in having no destination.

4

Throw over the jaws of it all, and good fortune will prevail. Stare into it with the wild-eyed gaze of a tiger full of slashing hunger and setting out on the hunt, and you never go astray.

5

Sweep its enduring loom-threads away, abide inexhaustible in dwelling, and good fortune will prevail. You cannot cross a great river.

6

From the jaws of it all comes affliction and good fortune. Crossing a great river brings forth wild bounty.

VAST BEYOND

Under the vast beyond, the roof's ridgepole sags. And so, setting out toward a destination brings forth wild bounty penetrating everywhere.

PRESENTATION

Vast beyond is everything beyond the vast. *The roof's ridgepole sags* because it's frail from end to end.

In that beyond, steely as a mountain in cloud, you inhabit the abiding center of things, moving there all reverent and inward, opening and delight.

Setting out toward a destination brings forth wild bounty: that is *penetrating everywhere.*

How vast, how utterly vast it is: the vast beyond following its proper seasons!

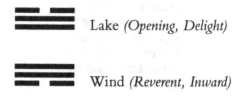 Lake *(Opening, Delight)*

Wind *(Reverent, Inward)*

IMAGE

A tree of wind engulfed beneath lake waters: that is *Vast Beyond.* Using it, the noble-minded stand alone without fear, and they use it to leave the peopled realm behind without remorse.

LINES

I

Use sun-white thatch-grass for sitting-mats, and you never go astray.

2

A derelict willow sends out new shoots. An aging man takes a young wife. How could that not bring forth wild bounty?

3

When the roof's ridgepole sags, calamity can't be far away.

4

When the roof's ridgepole is sturdy and high, good fortune prevails. But if you depend on empty gestures and artifice, your journey will be difficult indeed.

5

A derelict willow breaks into blossom. An aging woman takes a young husband. Though she's earned no praise, how has she gone astray?

6

In over your head crossing the river vast and beyond: it may bring calamity, but you'll never go astray.

ABIDING ABYSS

In the abiding abyss, possessing the dedication of a bird sitting on eggs: this is how heart-mind penetrates everywhere. Then, whatever you do, it will be revered.

PRESENTATION

The abiding abyss is all danger layered through danger. Water pours into it, but it's never filled. Can you inhabit that danger without losing your sincerity?

Heart-mind penetrates everywhere. This is to dwell at the abiding center of things, steely as a mountain in cloud.

Whatever you do, it will be revered. Setting out is where great achievement begins.

Heaven's danger is that you can't climb high enough. And earth's danger is rivers and mountains, hills and ridgelines.

Emperors and lords steep themselves in danger, and so protect their kingdoms.

Follow the seasons of danger, and you'll grow vast, so utterly vast indeed!

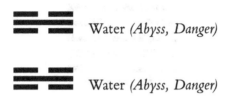 Water *(Abyss, Danger)*

Water *(Abyss, Danger)*

IMAGE

Where water flowing over and over settles: that is *Abiding Abyss*. Using it, the noble-minded move perennially with heart-sight clarity, abiding in the cultivation of their life's work.

LINES

I

In the abiding abyss, sunk into the shadow-cave abyss, you know calamity.

2

When the abyss is full of danger, look for small successes.

3

Coming and going is abyss after abyss. In that danger, caught there in that danger and sinking into the shadow-cave abyss: don't let it happen!

4

Wine in pots, grain in baskets, food in clay bowls: offer them through a window during adversity. In the end, how could you go astray?

5

In the abyss never full, the earth-spirit brims over. And so, nothing goes astray.

6

Bound in ropes and cords, stuck in a thorn-bramble prison for three years failing to get free: calamity has come.

RADIANCE

Inexhaustible and penetrating everywhere, radiance brings forth wild bounty. Nurture it like the docile strength of an ox, and good fortune will prevail.

PRESENTATION

Radiance is all beauty, beauty of heaven's sun and moon, beauty of the land's hundred grains and grasses and trees.

Sun and moon, fire and fire—using the beauty at the hinge of things, they transform and perfect all beneath heaven. And because the tender assent of this beauty is centered at the very hinge of things, it penetrates everywhere. And so: *nurture it like the docile strength of an ox, and good fortune will prevail.*

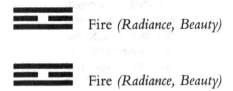

Fire *(Radiance, Beauty)*

Fire *(Radiance, Beauty)*

IMAGE

Sun and moon, fire and fire—they engender *Radiance*. Using it,
a great sage illuminates everything to the four corners of the world
with fiery light.

LINES

1

Walk in veneration, in reverence, and you never go astray.

2

Radiance of yellow, color of the earth: that is the origin of good
fortune.

3

If we do not drum and sing in the fading radiance of a setting sun,
what is there but the mourning cries of elders grown old? Calamity
thrives like that.

4

It seems so sudden—seems our arrival, seems our burning, seems our
death and abandonment.

5

Set out as if tears were falling, as if mourning cries were rising, then
good fortune will prevail.

6

If the emperor sets out like that with his armies, he can rejoice in
cutting off heads and seizing those who rebel against our own. If he
sets out like that, how could he go astray?

WHOLENESS

Penetrating everywhere, wholeness is inexhaustible in bringing forth wild bounty. Taking a woman in marriage brings forth good fortune.

PRESENTATION

Wholeness is what incites. Tender assent above and steely as a mountain in cloud below, *yin* above and *yang* below: it is through wholeness that these two *ch'i*-forces incite each other and move together.

Wholeness is abiding and delight, male beneath female—that's why *penetrating everywhere, wholeness is inexhaustible in bringing forth wild bounty, why taking a woman in marriage brings forth good fortune.*

When wholeness incites all heaven and earth, the ten thousand things are alive and all transformation.

When a great sage incites the people's heart-mind, all beneath heaven lives in tranquil accord.

If you can see what incites it all with a heron's-eye gaze, you are looking into the very nature of heaven and earth and the ten thousand things themselves.

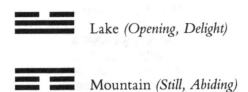

Lake *(Opening, Delight)*

Mountain *(Still, Abiding)*

IMAGE

Above mountains, a lake: that is *Wholeness*. Using it, the noble-minded welcome people with emptiness.

LINES

1

Wholeness fills your toes.

2

Wholeness fills your calves. You dwell calmly when calamity comes; and so, good fortune prevails.

3

Wholeness fills your thighs. Keeping faith with succession, all that will follow you, you set out through difficult journeys.

4

If you move with inexhaustible assurance, you come to good fortune and regret nothing. But if you wander back and forth, wavering and unsettled, your friends must worry over your every thought.

5

Wholeness fills your neck and spine. You live free of regret.

6

Wholeness fills your jaws and cheeks and the tongue that speaks.

MOONDRIFT CONSTANCY

Penetrating everywhere and never going astray, moondrift constancy
is inexhaustible in bringing forth wild bounty. Setting out toward
a destination brings forth wild bounty indeed.

PRESENTATION

Moondrift constancy endures on and on, all tender assent below and
steely as a mountain in cloud above. It is thunder moving together with
wind, the dragon's inciting force moving together with the reverent
and inward. Tender assent, steely as a mountain in cloud: moondrift
constancy is the two of them in concurrence.

*Penetrating everywhere and never going astray, moondrift constancy is
inexhaustible in bringing forth wild bounty.* This is to endure on and on
inhabiting your own Way. The Way of heaven and earth, too, is all
moondrift constancy enduring on and on without end.

Setting out toward a destination brings forth wild bounty indeed.
This is to find in every end a new beginning.

Sun and moon took to the sky, and so their radiance endures on and
on. The four seasons change and change, and so their completion
endures on and on. Great sages endure on and on inhabiting the Way
of moondrift constancy, and so all beneath heaven is transformed
into completion.

See moondrift constancy with a heron's-eye gaze, and you see
into the very nature of heaven and earth and the ten thousand
things themselves.

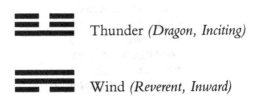

Thunder *(Dragon, Inciting)*

Wind *(Reverent, Inward)*

IMAGE
Thunder and wind: that is *Moondrift Constancy.* Using it, the noble-minded stand firm and never lose their direction.

LINES
I

If moondrift constancy is deep enough, it is inexhaustible even through calamity. If it's deep enough, there's wild bounty in having no destination.

2

What could there be to regret?

3

Practice heart-sight clarity constant as moondrift, or you'll learn to accept shame. And the difficulties of your journey will be inexhaustible indeed.

4

Fields empty of wild game.

5

Heart-sight clarity constant as moondrift, and inexhaustible: for a wife it brings good fortune, for a husband calamity.

6

Restlessness constant as moondrift: that always brings calamity.

33

SOLITUDE

Penetrating everywhere, solitude is inexhaustible in bringing forth very little bounty.

PRESENTATION

Penetrating everywhere, solitude is inexhaustible. In solitude, you penetrate everywhere, occupying a potent place steely as a mountain in cloud, concurring there with all things and moving according to your proper seasons.

Inexhaustible in bringing forth very little bounty. And so, you grow wise by brimming gradually out into flood.

How vast, how utterly vast it is: the meaning of solitude following its proper seasons!

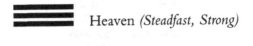 Heaven *(Steadfast, Strong)*

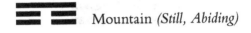 Mountain *(Still, Abiding)*

IMAGE

Throughout all beneath heaven, mountains: that is *Solitude.* Using it, the noble-minded keep clear of small-minded people—not in dislike for them, but in dignity.

LINES

I

When solitude ends, there's affliction. That's no way to set out toward a destination.

2

Bound in strips of skin that an ox shed, strips dyed yellow, color of earth, no one can break free.

3

Cling to solitude, and you find longing and affliction. Nurture sage-advisors, and good fortune will prevail.

4

Loving solitude, the noble-minded come to good fortune. But for the small-minded, solitude is mere obstruction.

5

Honor solitude, and good fortune will be inexhaustible indeed.

6

Enrich solitude, and there is no bounty it will not bring forth.

VAST POWER

Vast power is inexhaustible in bringing forth wild bounty.

PRESENTATION

Vast power is the vast full of power. It's power that comes from being steely as a mountain in cloud and using the dragon's inciting force.

Vast power is inexhaustible in bringing forth wild bounty. This is the vast abiding at the hinge of things. Vast at the hinge of things, you can see into the very nature of all heaven and earth!

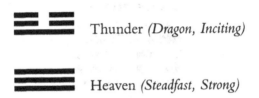

Thunder *(Dragon, Inciting)*

Heaven *(Steadfast, Strong)*

IMAGE

Thunder high in the heavens: that is *Vast Power*. Using it, the noble-minded walk always in veneration.

LINES

I

When there's power only in your feet, you forge ahead into calamity with the dedication of a bird sitting on eggs.

2

Good fortune inexhaustible indeed.

3

The small-minded use power. The noble-minded use nothing, and so move inexhaustible through affliction. A goat charging into a hedge is soon caught, its horns tangled tight.

4

Use nothing and good fortune is inexhaustible indeed. Then you live free of regret, and you break through the hedge without getting tangled. It's in the axle-bearing that the power of a vast cart resides.

5

Lose the goat in this ceaseless transformation of change. Then you live free of regret.

6

A charging goat caught in a hedge can't back out and can't push through. There's wild bounty in having no destination. Good fortune comes of difficulty.

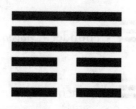

ADVANCEMENT

Advancement is when a sage advising peace and prosperity is given horses in large numbers and meets the emperor three times a day.

PRESENTATION

Advancement is moving ahead as an offering, is sun and moon rising above the earth, yielding and devoted as a river, all radiance and beauty vast in their illumination. All tender assent moving ahead, you move through ascendance as an offering. This is why *a sage advising peace and prosperity is given horses in large numbers and meets the emperor three times a day.*

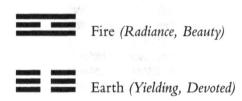

Fire *(Radiance, Beauty)*

Earth *(Yielding, Devoted)*

IMAGE
Sun and moon rising all vast illumination above the earth: that is
Advancement. Using it, the noble-minded illuminate their heart-sight
clarity.

LINES
I
Inexhaustible in advancement and inexhaustible in reversal, you come
to good fortune. If you can depend on nothing with the dedication
of a bird sitting on eggs, you'll be enriched and never go astray.
2
Inexhaustible in advancement and inexhaustible in grief, you
come to good fortune, receiving blessings and prosperity from the
Ancestral Mother.
3
Trust everything. What could there be to regret?
4
Industrious as a squirrel in advancement, you move inexhaustible
through affliction.
5
What could there be to regret? Don't worry over failure and success,
then setting out will bring good fortune indeed. And how could it not
bring forth wild bounty?
6
If you depend on horns for advancement, all you can do is attack a city.
Find good fortune coming of affliction, and you never go astray.
The difficulties of your journey will be inexhaustible indeed.

36

ILLUMINATION BLACKENED

When illumination is blackened, move inexhaustible through difficulty and you'll find wild bounty.

PRESENTATION

Sun and moon sinking all vast illumination below the earth: that is *Illumination Blackened*. Inside that illumination at the grain of things, outside all tender assent yielding and devoted as a river: let that carry you through the inception-thicket of vast troubles. That's how Emperor Wen did it.

Move inexhaustible through difficulty and you'll find wild bounty. When illumination is darkened over, it can still center your purpose at the hinge of things, even if your troubles lie deep within. That's how Lord Winnow did it.

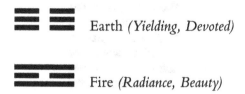

Earth *(Yielding, Devoted)*

Fire *(Radiance, Beauty)*

IMAGE

Sun and moon sinking all vast illumination below the earth: that is
Illumination Blackened. Using it, the noble-minded guide the people.
And they use darkness to abide in illumination itself.

LINES

I

Illumination blackened in flight, you fold your wings. The noble-
minded journey three days without eating. They set out toward a
destination where there's a master offering wise counsel.

2

Illumination blackened wounds the left thigh, but carried by the saving
power of a horse, you come to good fortune.

3

Illumination blackened at war in the solar southlands, they take the
great chief captive. If you're inexhaustible, you can't be full of
anxious longing.

4

Enter the left side of the belly and inhabit your inner powers. Then,
anytime you leave your courtyard gate, you carry the heart-mind of
illumination blackened.

5

Lord Winnow's illumination was blackened, but he remained
inexhaustible in bringing forth wild bounty.

6

In darkness lacking all illumination, you ascend first into heaven, then
sink into earth.

FAMILY
With inexhaustible women, family brings forth wild bounty.

PRESENTATION
In family, a woman inhabits the hinge of things, finding her potent place within. And a man too inhabits the hinge of things, finding his potent place without. Man and woman inhabiting the hinge of things together: in this lies the vast meaning of all heaven and earth.

Family has its stern rulers, and they're called the mother and father.

When father is altogether father and child child, brother brother and sister sister, husband husband and wife wife—the Way of family moves at the hinge of things. Keep your family at the hinge of things, and all beneath heaven will be settled in its proper order.

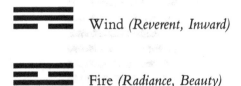

Wind *(Reverent, Inward)*

Fire *(Radiance, Beauty)*

IMAGE

Wind emerging from fire: that is *Family*. Using it, the noble-minded invest their words with the lived substance of things themselves, and they invest their actions with moondrift constancy.

LINES

I

Defend home and family, and you'll regret nothing.

2

Don't set out imagining distant destinations. Stay home, and you can push through to completion, for the nourishment of the abiding center is inexhaustible in bringing forth good fortune.

3

If the family is clear and disciplined, there may be regrets, but good fortune will come of any affliction. If wife and child are all chit and giggling chat, it will be a difficult journey indeed.

4

A home enriched brings forth vast good fortune.

5

If the emperor stays close to home and family, he need not worry. Good fortune will prevail.

6

Nurture the dedication of a bird sitting on eggs, make it majestic, and good fortune endures whole and through to completion.

DIFFERENCE
Even in small matters, difference brings forth good fortune.

PRESENTATION
In their difference, fire rises above with the dragon's inciting force, and lake sinks below with the dragon's inciting force.

When two women live together, it's a give and take of wills never moving together.

All opening and delight, radiance and beauty, you abide in illumination. All tender assent moving ahead, you move through ascendance as an offering. And inhabiting the abiding center, you concur with everything steely as a mountain in cloud. This is how *even in small matters, difference brings forth good fortune.*

Heaven and earth are different, but their purposes are the same. Man and woman are different, but their aspirations open through one another. The ten thousand things are different, but their purposes are always kindred.

Follow the seasons of difference, and you'll grow vast, so utterly vast indeed!

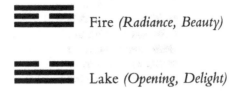

Fire *(Radiance, Beauty)*

Lake *(Opening, Delight)*

IMAGE

Fire above and lake below: that is *Difference*. Using it, the noble-minded
understand how sameness becomes variation.

LINES

1

What could there be to regret? Don't chase a lost horse, and it will
return on its own. Watch the people who do evil, and you'll never
go astray.

2

Meet the master in a narrow lane. How could you ever go astray?

3

Watch the star-cart trailed out behind—oxen struggling, drivers
branded with the tattoos and missing noses of criminals. Never begin,
and you've come to completion.

4

In difference, we are alone. Those who meet at origins are woven
together in the dedication of a bird sitting on eggs. Even in affliction,
they never go astray.

5

What could there be to regret? The ancestral source feeds on flesh. If
you set out, how could you ever go astray?

6

In difference, we are alone. Watch the pig-star covered in mud, the
star-cart carrying ghosts. First bow-stars drawn, then bow-stars
unstrung. Never a thief marry. If you encounter rain upon setting out,
good fortune will prevail.

ADVERSITY

In adversity, there's wild bounty on southwest plains and no bounty in northeast mountains. Seeking advice from a great sage brings forth wild bounty and good fortune inexhaustible indeed.

PRESENTATION

Adversity is troubles, is danger to face. If you can stop short when you see danger, you are wise, wise indeed!

In adversity, there's wild bounty on southwest plains, because going there you inhabit the abiding center of things. There is *no bounty in northeast mountains*, because there the Way withers exhausted away.

Seeking advice from a great sage brings forth wild bounty. Setting out is where great achievement begins.

Find a potent place, make good fortune inexhaustible there, and you can center the nation at the very hinge of things.

Follow the seasons of adversity, and you'll grow vast, so utterly vast indeed!

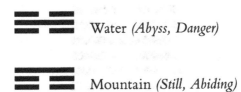

Water *(Abyss, Danger)*

Mountain *(Still, Abiding)*

IMAGE

Above mountains, water: that is *Adversity*. Using it, the noble-minded turn back within themselves and cultivate heart-sight clarity.

LINES

1

In setting out, there's adversity. In arriving, there's acclaim.

2

An emperor's sage-advisors face adversity after adversity, and it's never for their own gain.

3

In setting out, there's adversity. In arriving, there's return.

4

In setting out, there's adversity. In arriving, there's connection.

5

In the midst of great adversity, friends arrive.

6

In setting out, there's adversity. In arriving, there's eminence and good fortune. Seeking advice from a great sage brings forth wild bounty.

UNBOUND

On southwest plains, wild bounty is unbound. Set out with nowhere to go, and returning home brings good fortune indeed. Set out toward a destination, and dawn brings good fortune indeed.

PRESENTATION

Unbound in the face of danger, you can use the dragon's inciting force. Using the dragon's inciting force to elude danger: that is the unbound.

On southwest plains, wild bounty is unbound because going there you abide with the people.

Returning home brings good fortune because you inhabit the abiding center of things.

Set out toward a destination, and dawn brings good fortune indeed. Setting out is where great achievement begins.

When heaven and earth come unbound, thunder and rain break loose. When thunder and rain break loose, the hundred fruits and wildflowers and trees all burst into life.

How vast, how utterly vast it is: the unbound following its proper seasons.

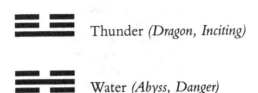

Thunder *(Dragon, Inciting)*

Water *(Abyss, Danger)*

IMAGE

Thunder and rain breaking loose: that is *Unbound*. Using it, the noble-minded forgive mistakes and pardon crimes.

LINES

I

Without going astray.

2

Capture three secretive foxes out in the fields, find an arrow painted yellow, color of earth: good fortune will be inexhaustible indeed.

3

Ride along with a treasure mounted on your back, and bandits will soon arrive. The difficulties of your journey will be inexhaustible indeed.

4

When you're unbound and thumbing defiance, friends come with the dedication of a bird sitting on eggs.

5

The noble-minded alone master the unbound. The dedication of a bird sitting on eggs: if you can sustain it in the face of small-minded people, good fortune will prevail.

6

When lords use it to shoot down hawks atop high city walls, or to capture them, there is no bounty it does not bring forth.

DEPLETION

If you master depletion, you find the dedication of a bird sitting on eggs, find all origins bringing forth good fortune. Never going astray, you move inexhaustible indeed. And so, setting out toward a destination brings forth wild bounty. How can you use depletion? Make an offering with two simple baskets, and it penetrates everywhere.

PRESENTATION

Depletion depletes the lowly and enriches the lofty: such is the Way in its lofty movement.

Master depletion, then *you find the dedication of a bird sitting on eggs, find all origins bringing forth good fortune. Never going astray, you move inexhaustible indeed. And so, setting out toward a destination brings forth wild bounty.*

How can you use depletion? Make an offering with two simple baskets, and it penetrates everywhere. Those two simple baskets concur with the proper seasons. Depletion steely as a mountain in cloud, enrichment all tender assent: they follow their proper seasons. Depletion and enrichment, empty and full: they all move together according to their proper seasons.

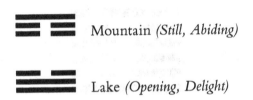

Mountain *(Still, Abiding)*

Lake *(Opening, Delight)*

IMAGE

Below mountains, a lake: that is *Depletion*. Using it, the noble-minded resolve anger and restrain desire.

LINES

1

Move on quickly when the task is finished, then you never go astray. Move on with depletion always in mind.

2

You may be inexhaustible in wild bounty, but setting out will bring calamity. Don't deplete things. Enrich them.

3

When three people travel together, they're soon depleted by one person. If you travel alone, you soon gain a friend.

4

Deplete anxious longing, and you'll soon find joy. How could you go astray then?

5

Enrich depletion with the wisdom in ten paired strings of oracle-bones, and who could oppose it? There, you dwell at the very origins of good fortune.

6

Don't deplete things. Enrich them. Then, you'll never go astray and good fortune will be inexhaustible indeed. Setting out toward a destination brings forth wild bounty indeed, for you won't find a sage-advisor at home.

ENRICHMENT

If you master enrichment, setting out toward a destination brings forth wild bounty and crossing a great river brings forth wild bounty.

PRESENTATION

Enrichment depletes everything lofty and enriches everything lowly, so the people's joy swells beyond all bounds. Everything lofty sinking beneath everything lowly: such is the Way in its vast radiance.

Setting out toward a destination brings forth wild bounty. Centered at the hinge of things, you know blessings.

Crossing a great river brings forth wild bounty. The Way of boat-timber trees is what makes it possible.

Enrichment is the dragon's inciting force moving together with the reverent and inward. In enrichment, you move ahead as an offering, on and on and beyond all bounds.

Heaven bestows, earth begets, and so enrichment continues always and everywhere. The Way of enrichment moves always in accord with its proper seasons.

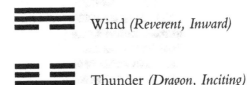

Wind *(Reverent, Inward)*

Thunder *(Dragon, Inciting)*

IMAGE

Wind and thunder: that is *Enrichment*. Using it, the noble-minded recognize wholeness and perfect it, recognize trespass and transform it.

LINES

I

Use enrichment in great undertakings, and wild bounty will prevail. There, you dwell at the very origins of good fortune. How could you ever go astray?

2

Enrich enrichment with the wisdom in ten paired strings of oracle-bones, and who could oppose it? It's all perennial good fortune inexhaustible indeed. When emperors used it, they penetrated everywhere making summer offerings to the Celestial Lord, and good fortune prevailed.

3

Use enrichment when calamity comes, and you'll never go astray. Possess the dedication of a bird sitting on eggs, and you move at the abiding center of things. Then you're worthy of carrying a jade amulet and advising a lord.

4

If you inhabit the abiding center of things, the lord you advise will trust and follow you. Rely on enrichment to transform the nation, and wild bounty will prevail.

5

From the dedication of a bird sitting on eggs comes a heart-mind all kindness and generosity. Give up questions, and you dwell at the very origins of good fortune. From the dedication of a bird sitting on eggs comes my heart-sight clarity all kindness and generosity.

6

People don't enrich enrichment, and some attack it. Establish a heart-mind without moondrift constancy, and you'll soon know calamity.

RESOLUTE

If you're resolute, you speak openly at the emperor's court, you cry out with the dedication of a bird sitting on eggs, even if it brings affliction. Sentinels call from city walls. An attack would bring forth no bounty. Setting out toward a destination brings forth wild bounty indeed.

PRESENTATION

Resolute is to break through and clear away, is steely as a mountain in cloud all tender assent breaking through and clearing away. It's steadfast and strong, opening and delight. It breaks through and clears away, perfecting harmony.

If you're resolute, you speak openly at the emperor's court. A line of tender assent here rides atop five lines steely as a mountain in cloud.

You cry out with the dedication of a bird sitting on eggs, even if it brings affliction. When you risk peril like that, you come into radiance.

Sentinels call from city walls. An attack would bring forth no bounty. Whatever rises up eventually withers exhausted away.

Setting out toward a destination brings forth wild bounty indeed. If you're strong and steely as a mountain in cloud, you endure whole and through to completion.

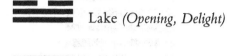

43

Lake *(Opening, Delight)*

Heaven *(Steadfast, Strong)*

IMAGE

A lake floating above heaven: that is *Resolute.* Using it, the noble-minded spread blessings among the lowly. Abiding in heart-sight clarity, they know what to avoid.

LINES

I

When there's power only in your feet moving ahead, you set out but can't avoid going astray.

2

When there are sentinels to cry out warnings deep in the night, the city doesn't worry about attack.

3

When there's power only in your cheekbone, calamity can't be far away. The noble-minded are resolute, always resolute. They walk alone, endure drenching rains. And even full of resentment, they never go astray.

4

Haunches without flesh never walk far. They soon falter. Lead the sheep along, and there will be nothing to regret. Listen to talk, and you hear no sincerity, no accuracy.

5

A gardener vigilant against weeds is resolute, always resolute. Move at the abiding center of things, and you never go astray.

6

Without warning cries, there will be calamity whole and through to completion.

GENERATIVE

The generative is woman's power. And so it is that a woman isn't something you can simply seize and use.

PRESENTATION

The generative is everything occurring, is tender assent occurring steely as a mountain in cloud.

A woman isn't something you can simply seize and use, for when you seize something you cannot keep it for long.

Heaven and earth occur together, and so the intricate array of things appears, whole in its beauty.

Centered at the hinge of things and steely as a mountain in cloud, it all occurs. That is the movement of all beneath heaven, and it is vast.

How vast, how utterly vast it is: the meaning of the generative following its proper seasons!

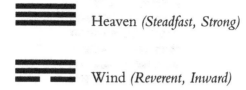 Heaven *(Steadfast, Strong)*

Wind *(Reverent, Inward)*

IMAGE

Wind stirring throughout all beneath heaven: that is *Generative*. Using it, Mother-Empress opens the inevitable unfurling of things far and wide, and so commands everything to the four corners of the world.

LINES

1

If you're governed by metal brakes, good fortune will be inexhaustible indeed. But if you simply set out toward a destination, you will know calamity. A starved pig has all the dedication of a bird sitting on eggs as it wanders around in confusion.

2

If you keep fish stored in famine-willow wrappers, you never go astray. There's no bounty in guests.

3

Haunches without flesh never walk far. They soon falter. Even in affliction, you'll never go seriously astray.

4

If you don't keep fish stored in famine-willow wrappers, calamity has come.

5

A gourd wrapped in famine-willow. Harbor beauty within, then all failure and defeat comes from heaven alone.

6

When the generative shows its horns, the journey gets difficult, but you never go astray.

COMPOSURE

In composure you penetrate everywhere, like a true emperor staying close to the temple. Seeking advice from a great sage brings forth wild bounty, and it penetrates everywhere, inexhaustible in bringing forth wild bounty. Offer great beasts when you sacrifice, and good fortune will prevail. Setting out toward a destination brings forth wild bounty indeed.

PRESENTATION

Composure is everything gathered together. Opening and delight, yielding and devoted as a river, you abide centered as a steely mountain in cloud. In this you concur with all things, abide in everything gathered together.

A true emperor staying close to the temple penetrates everywhere by honoring the ancestors.

Seeking advice from a great sage brings forth wild bounty, and it penetrates everywhere. It's everything gathered together at the hinge of things.

Offer great beasts when you sacrifice, and good fortune will prevail. Setting out toward a destination brings forth wild bounty indeed. Such is the inevitable unfurling of heaven, heaven yielding and devoted as a river.

See everything gathered together with a heron's-eye gaze, and you see into the very nature of heaven and earth and the ten thousand things themselves.

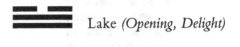 Lake *(Opening, Delight)*

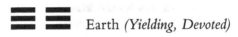 Earth *(Yielding, Devoted)*

IMAGE

A lake floating above earth: that is *Composure*. Using it, the noble-minded keep the tools of war in constant readiness, and so guard against disaster.

LINES

I

If you don't sustain the dedication of a bird sitting on eggs, if you don't sustain it whole and through to completion, things will sometimes be scattered and sometimes composed. If there are sentinels to cry out warning, the city can hold fast to laughter and never worry about attack. If you set out, you won't go astray.

2

Draw good fortune like a bow, and you'll never go astray. Offer even a simple spring sacrifice of wildflowers with the dedication of a bird sitting on eggs, and wild bounty will prevail.

3

Move with composure, with awe in wonder, and there's wild bounty in having no destination. If you set out, you won't go astray, and the difficulties of your journey will be few.

4

Good fortune is vast. You'll never go astray.

5

Composed in a potent place, you never go astray. Forget the dedication of a bird sitting on eggs. When origins go on forever, inexhaustible forever, what could there be to regret?

6

You might cry and sob in lament, but you'll never go astray.

46

ASCENT

In their ascent, origins penetrate everywhere. Wield that ascent when
seeking advice from a great sage, and there's no need to worry. Set out
for the south, and good fortune will prevail.

PRESENTATION

Use the seasons of ascent with tender assent, then you'll abide centered
as a steely mountain in cloud: reverent and inward, yielding and
devoted as a river. In this you'll concur with all things, move vast and
penetrating everywhere.

*Wield that ascent when seeking advice from a great sage, and there's no need to
worry,* for it will bring blessings.

Set out for the south, and good fortune will prevail, for your purposes
will be realized.

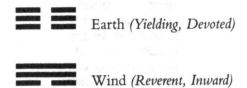

Earth *(Yielding, Devoted)*

Wind *(Reverent, Inward)*

IMAGE

A tree of wind born at the earth's abiding center: that is *Ascent*.
Using it, the noble-minded abide in heart-sight clarity, always yielding
and devoted as a river. They use it to make everyday little things
lofty and vast.

LINES

I

Trust ascent, and good fortune will be vast indeed.

2

If you offer even a simple spring sacrifice of wildflowers with the
dedication of a bird sitting on eggs, wild bounty will prevail.
How could you ever go astray?

3

Ascent into an empty city.

4

Wielding ascent, Emperor T'ai penetrated everywhere through to
Bowhand Mountain. And so we knew good fortune and never went
astray.

5

In inexhaustible good fortune, ascent comes step by step.

6

The ascent of shadowy mystery: inexhaustible and without rest, it
brings forth wild bounty.

EXHAUSTION

In exhaustion penetrating everywhere, a great sage is inexhaustible,
bringing forth good fortune and never going astray. When there's talk,
there's no sincerity, no accuracy.

PRESENTATION

In exhaustion, the noble-minded are hemmed in and steely as a
mountain in cloud. They master opening and delight amid danger. In
exhaustion, they never lose those depths that penetrate everywhere.
Isn't that what makes them noble-minded?

A great sage is inexhaustible, bringing forth good fortune, for he is centered as
a steely mountain in cloud.

When there's talk, there's no sincerity, no accuracy. Revere words, and you
soon wither impoverished away.

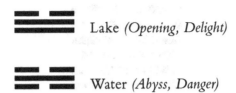 Lake *(Opening, Delight)*

Water *(Abyss, Danger)*

IMAGE

A lake without water: that is *Exhaustion*. Using it, the noble-minded abide in the inevitable unfurling of things and keep faith with its purposes.

LINES

1

Haunches in exhaustion among tree roots, you enter a valley all shadowy mystery, and no one sees you for three years.

2

In exhaustion among food and drink, you receive crimson robes. Wear them in sacrificial ceremony penetrating everywhere, and wild bounty will prevail. Set out and calamity may come, but you'll never go astray.

3

In exhaustion scrambling up rock, you grasp at pear-thorn vines. If a man returns home and doesn't see his wife, calamity has come.

4

Coming slow and regal in exhaustion among metal war-carts, it's a difficult journey whole and through to completion.

5

You may have nose and feet lopped off for crimes committed, but in exhaustion among scarlet robes, you'll come slowly to joy. Wear them in sacrificial ceremony, and wild bounty will prevail.

6

In exhaustion among bramble-vines, among dizzy anxieties, tell yourself this: *To act brings regret. But even if there's regret, setting out will bring good fortune indeed.*

WELL

You can move the city, but not the well. It never loses, and it never gains. People come and go, but the well remains a well. But if it's a well drained dry, if it's a well without a rope, or the jug is broken, calamity can't be far away.

PRESENTATION

A reverent and inward wind meeting the abyss and danger of water: the well is where you raise that water up.

You can move the city, but not the well, for the well is centered as a steely mountain in cloud.

If it's a well drained dry, if it's a well without a rope, it can achieve nothing.

The jug is broken. That's what brings calamity.

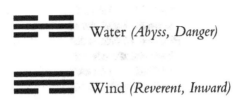

Water *(Abyss, Danger)*

Wind *(Reverent, Inward)*

IMAGE

Water above a tree of wind: that is the *Well*. Using it, the noble-minded inspire the people to work together.

LINES

1

When the well turns to mud, you can't drink there. Not even birds bother with an old well like that.

2

In a valley with wells, you can shoot fish. If a water-jar leaks, it's worn out.

3

When the well turns rancid, and no one drinks, it fills my heart-mind with remorse. It's so easy to draw water. And when an emperor is illuminated in wisdom, joy and prosperity rain down on everyone together.

4

Line your well with brick, and you'll never go astray.

5

When the well holds springwater cold and crystal-pure, drink deeply.

6

The well's bounty isn't hidden away. If you come with the dedication of a bird sitting on eggs, you'll find in it the very origins of good fortune.

49

SHEDDING SKIN

On the days of their demise, reinventing themselves with the dedication of a bird sitting on eggs, things shed skins. That's how it is. All origins penetrating everywhere, heaven is inexhaustible in bringing forth wild bounty. What could there be to regret?

PRESENTATION

Shedding skin is an endless process: water drowning fire, fire parching water.

When two women live together, that give and take of wills: it's called *shedding skin*.

On the days of their demise, reinventing themselves with the dedication of a bird sitting on eggs, things shed skins. Shedding skin, you move with sincerity. You use opening and delight to inhabit that illumination at the grain of things, and you use the hinge of things to penetrate everywhere throughout the wild vastness of things.

When shedding skin is proper and right, what could there be to regret? Heaven and earth keep shedding skins, and so the four seasons come to completion.

Shedding skin according to the inevitable unfurling of things, emperors T'ang and Wu were yielding and devoted as a river in following heaven and concurring with the people.

How vast, how utterly vast it is: the shedding of skin following its proper seasons!

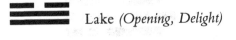

Lake *(Opening, Delight)*

Fire *(Radiance, Beauty)*

IMAGE

Fire at the lake's abiding center: that is *Shedding Skin*. Using it, the noble-minded put the calendar in order and illuminate the proper seasons.

LINES

1

To lash things tight, use strips of skin that an ox shed, strips dyed yellow, color of earth.

2

On the days of their demise, things move on by shedding skins. And so, setting forth will bring good fortune indeed. How could you ever go astray?

3

Setting forth will bring calamity inexhaustible in affliction. Shed the skin of words three times over, and you master the dedication of a bird sitting on eggs.

4

What could there be to regret? Possess the dedication of a bird sitting on eggs, and you'll find good fortune in the inevitable unfurling of things, all that transfiguration.

5

Great sages are tigers all transformation through and through. Before divination, we had the dedication of a bird sitting on eggs.

6

The noble-minded are leopards all transformation through and through. The small-minded are all about appearances. That's the only skin they can shed. Setting forth will bring calamity. Stay home, and good fortune will be inexhaustible indeed.

CAULDRON

Cauldron is the very origin of good fortune. It penetrates everywhere.

PRESENTATION

Cauldron is the *Image*.

Heated by the reverent and inward tree of wind burning with the radiance and beauty of fire, cauldron penetrates everywhere, cooking things through and through.

Great sages long ago penetrated everywhere—for when they used cauldron, the Celestial Lord penetrated everywhere. And now, vast and penetrating everywhere, cauldron nurtures great sages and wise elders.

It's because you possess cauldron's reverent and inward tree of burning wind that eye and ear know light and sound. And possessing its fire, you move all tender assent through ascendance as an offering. You come to the abiding center of things, and move always in concurrence with everything steely as a mountain in cloud. That is how you penetrate all origins everywhere.

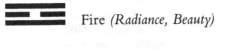 Fire *(Radiance, Beauty)*

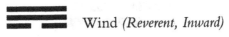 Wind *(Reverent, Inward)*

IMAGE

Above a tree of wind, fire: that is *Cauldron*. Using it, the noble-minded inhabit a potent place at the hinge of things, where the inevitable unfurling of things comes to pass.

LINES

1

When cauldron is tipped feet upward, things emerge from obstruction, bringing forth wild bounty. In love, think of the children to come, and you never go astray.

2

When cauldron is full, my enemies grow sick and cannot hinder me, then good fortune prevails.

3

Cauldron sheds its ears in the shedding of skin, and without ears it can't be moved, so no one dines on rich pheasant meat. But rain soon arrives, rinsing regret away, and good fortune opens whole and through to completion.

4

When cauldron's leg is broken, it spills out the stew of lords, drenching their shadows. Calamity has come.

5

When cauldron has rings of gold enigma and ears of yellow, color of the earth, it's inexhaustible in bringing forth wild bounty.

6

When cauldron has rings of jade enigma, it brings forth vast good fortune. How could there not be wild bounty everywhere?

THUNDER

Thunder penetrates everywhere. Thunder comes bringing terror, sheer terror; and that's the time to laugh and talk, cackle and caw. Thunder startles everything, even from a hundred miles away, without jostling a drop from the ladle of sacrificial wine.

PRESENTATION

Thunder penetrates everywhere. Thunder comes bringing terror, sheer terror. Fear is what leads to joy and prosperity.

And that's the time to laugh and talk, cackle and caw. Later on, rules and laws will appear.

Thunder startles everything, even from a hundred miles away. To be startled from a distance means dread is close at hand.

When thunder emerges, why not use it to guard over ancestral temples and earth altars? Why not use it to preside over offerings and ceremonies there?

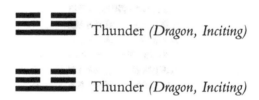

Thunder *(Dragon, Inciting)*

Thunder *(Dragon, Inciting)*

IMAGE

Dragon flowing over and under: that is *Thunder*. Using it, the noble-minded examine and cultivate themselves by living with fear and dread.

LINES

1

Thunder comes bringing terror, sheer terror; and that's the time to laugh and talk, cackle and caw. In this, good fortune prevails.

2

Thunder comes bringing affliction, enough to plunder your treasure a hundred thousand times over. Climb nine ridgelines, wander there looking for nothing, and after seven days you'll understand.

3

Thunder brings dread, such deep dread. It roams and roams and does no wrong.

4

When thunder comes, mud and mire follow.

5

Thunder comes and goes, bringing affliction a hundred thousand times over. It's never without work to do.

6

Thunder brings scattered ruin and spooked worry, eyes gazing around in panic, sheer panic. Setting forth will bring calamity. Even if thunder doesn't find you, it will find your neighbor. How could it ever go astray? And so, it turns marriage into haunted talk and more talk.

STILLNESS

Stillness in your back. Expect nothing from your life. Wander the courtyard where you see no one. How could you ever go astray?

PRESENTATION
Stillness is the same as abiding.

In the season for abiding, abide. In the season for moving, move.

If you take action in the proper season and cultivate quiet in the proper season, your Way is radiant with the illumination of sun and moon and the dragon's inciting force.

Stillness in abiding means abiding in whatever you are.

Lofty and lowly stand in opposition; they share nothing. This is why you never go astray when you *expect nothing from your life*, when you *wander the courtyard where you see no one*.

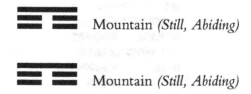

Mountain *(Still, Abiding)*

Mountain *(Still, Abiding)*

IMAGE

Two mountains in one: that is *Stillness*. Using it, the noble-minded master thought never leaving its potent place.

LINES

I

Stillness fills your feet. You never go astray, and wild bounty goes on inexhaustible and without end.

2

Stillness fills your calves. Raise up succession, all that will follow you, or you'll never know contentment.

3

Stillness fills your waist. It puts girdling muscles in order, and afflictions that cloud the heart-mind.

4

Stillness fills your body. How could you ever go astray?

5

Stillness fills your jaws and cheeks. Words come in their proper order. What could there be to regret?

6

Honor stillness, and you'll know good fortune.

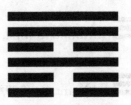

GRADUAL

It's gradual—the good fortune of a woman coming home in marriage,
that wild bounty inexhaustible indeed.

PRESENTATION

Gradual means moving ahead as an offering, means *the good fortune of a
woman coming home in marriage.*

To move ahead as an offering is to occupy a potent place, for setting
out is where great achievement begins. In that offering you use the
hinge of things, and so you can rectify the nation, returning it to
the hinge of things.

When you occupy a potent place steely as a mountain in cloud, you
inhabit the very center of things.

Still and abiding, reverent and inward: the dragon's inciting force is
never exhausted.

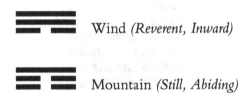

Wind *(Reverent, Inward)*

Mountain *(Still, Abiding)*

IMAGE
Above mountains, a tree of wind: that is *Gradual*. Using it, the noble-minded inhabit the heart-sight clarity of sage-elders, and so bring wholeness to the most ordinary of lives.

LINES
1

Migrating geese are gradual in coming to shorelines. Even a small child possesses the affliction of words. Nothing goes astray.

2

Migrating geese are gradual in coming to cliff-walls. Food and wine offer pleasure, such deep pleasure, and good fortune indeed.

3

Migrating geese are gradual in coming to plateaus. Husbands set forth, never to return. Wives conceive never to give birth. Resist tyrants and calamity comes, but so too does wild bounty.

4

Migrating geese are gradual in coming to a tree of wind. Some find their way in under rafters. Nothing goes astray.

5

Migrating geese are gradual in coming to ridgelines. Wives pass three years without conceiving. Nothing triumphs in the end, and that too brings forth good fortune.

6

Migrating geese are gradual in coming to plateaus. Learn to use their feathers in ritual and dance, and good fortune will prevail.

54

HOME IN MARRIAGE

Setting forth only brings calamity for a girl come home in marriage.
There's wild bounty in having no destination.

PRESENTATION

A girl come home in marriage: that is the vast meaning of all heaven and earth. If heaven and earth were not woven together, the ten thousand things would never burgeon forth into being and flourish.

A girl come home in marriage: that is the end and the beginning of humankind.

Moving with the dragon's inciting force all opening and delight: that's what *a girl come home in marriage* is.

Setting forth only brings calamity. Your potent place is not proper and right.

There's wild bounty in having no destination. Lines of tender assent here ride atop lines steely as a mountain in cloud.

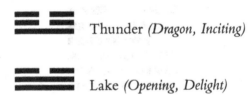

Thunder *(Dragon, Inciting)*

Lake *(Opening, Delight)*

IMAGE

Above a lake, thunder: that is *Home in Marriage.* Using it, the noble-minded understand it's death coming to everything that makes this world perpetual and whole through to completion.

LINES

I

A girl come home in marriage as a second wife. One leg lame, you can still walk. Setting out will bring good fortune indeed.

2

One eye gone, you can still see. There's wild bounty in the inexhaustible life of a recluse.

3

A girl come home in marriage by waiting. She returned, then came as a second wife.

4

A girl come home in marriage though past her prime. Even a late marriage has its proper season.

5

When a girl comes home in marriage to Lord Burgeon, she dresses in the kind of robes that lords wear, robes with sleeves less glamourous than those of a second wife. After a few full moons, good fortune comes.

6

Women offer baskets without fruit. Men sacrifice sheep without blood. There's wild bounty in having no destination.

ABUNDANCE

Abundance penetrates everywhere, a ritual vessel crowded with blossoms. A true emperor stays close to it, offers its ritual bloom. Live without worry, and you live in accord with the midday sun.

PRESENTATION

Abundance is vast indeed. Use dragon's inciting force to perfect sage illumination, and you master abundance with its ritual bloom.

A true emperor stays close to it, offers its ritual bloom, because he reveres the vast.

Live without worry, and you live in accord with the midday sun. That is to live in accord with the radiance flooding all beneath heaven.

The midday sun soon sets. The full moon soon wanes. Heaven and earth fill and empty, ebb and flow according to their proper seasons. And isn't this even more true for people, more true for ghosts and spirits?

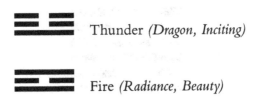

Thunder *(Dragon, Inciting)*

Fire *(Radiance, Beauty)*

IMAGE

Thunder and lightning joined together: that is *Abundance*. Using it, the noble-minded settle court cases and exact punishments.

LINES

I

Meet a kindred master. Pass ten days together. How could you go astray? Setting out, go in veneration.

2

When the ritual bloom of abundance spreads its veil, you can see the Big Dipper at midday. If you set out with doubt and suspicion, you will know anxious longing. If you set out with the dedication of a bird sitting on eggs, you will know good fortune.

3

When the ritual bloom of abundance spreads its curtain, you can see even faint stars at midday. You might break your right arm, but how could you go astray?

4

When the ritual bloom of abundance spreads its veil, you can see the Big Dipper at midday. Meet a foreign master, and good fortune will prevail.

5

Come revealing beauty all around you, and you'll know blessings and praise, and such good fortune.

6

When the ritual bloom of abundance fills your house, when it veils your home, gaze through doors into courtyards, still and quiet in your solitude. If you pass three years unseen like this, calamity has come.

WANDERING

Through wandering, you penetrate everywhere in the smallest ways; and so, wandering is good fortune inexhaustible indeed.

PRESENTATION

Through wandering, you penetrate everywhere in the smallest ways. All tender assent centered in the beyond, you move yielding and devoted as a river through everything steely as a mountain in cloud.

Still and abiding, radiance and beauty: if you use all this illumination, *you penetrate everywhere in the smallest ways; and so, wandering is good fortune inexhaustible indeed.*

How vast, how utterly vast it is: the meaning of wandering according to your proper seasons!

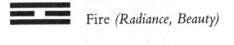 Fire *(Radiance, Beauty)*

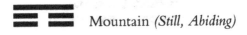 Mountain *(Still, Abiding)*

IMAGE
Above mountains, fire: that is *Wandering*. Using it, the noble-minded illuminate the caution needed to avoid long court cases and unnecessary punishments.

LINES
I
Wandering driven by cheap and petty distractions: that is how you choose disaster for yourself.

2
Wandering, you stop at an inn. Longing there for the rich comforts of home, you master the inexhaustible endurance of a servant.

3
Wandering, you burn down the inn and lose the inexhaustible endurance of servants. And it's pure affliction.

4
Wandering, you come to a resting place and use an ax to establish the rich comforts of home. But I'm never satisfied, never settled in joy.

5
Try shooting a pheasant, and you lose an arrow. Wandering whole and through to completion—that's how you praise the inevitable unfurling of things.

6
A bird burns down its nest. A wanderer laughs at first, but sobs and cries out in the end. Lose your ox to the onslaught of change, and calamity has come.

REVERENCE

Through inward reverence, you penetrate everywhere in the smallest ways. Setting out toward a destination brings forth wild bounty, and seeking advice from a great sage also brings forth wild bounty.

PRESENTATION

Inward reverence layered through reverence, that is how you further the inevitable unfolding of things.

If you live all inward reverence steely as a mountain in cloud, you live centered at the hinge of things, and your purposes will be realized.

All tender assent, you move yielding and devoted as a river through everything steely as a mountain in cloud. If you move like this, *you penetrate everywhere in the smallest ways.* If you move like this, *setting out toward a destination brings forth wild bounty, and seeking advice from a great sage also brings forth wild bounty.*

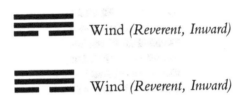

Wind *(Reverent, Inward)*

Wind *(Reverent, Inward)*

IMAGE

A succession of wind through wind: that is *Reverence*. Using it, the noble-minded further the inevitable unfolding of things, and so realize their life's work.

LINES

1

Through advances and setbacks, the inexhaustible endurance of a warrior brings forth wild bounty.

2

Reverence beneath reverence. Honor heaven and earth with priests and shamans, and there will be no end of good fortune. How could you ever go astray?

3

If reverence is harried and sullen, life is a difficult journey indeed.

4

What could there be to regret? Hunting the fields, you find quarry of every kind.

5

Good fortune is inexhaustible indeed. What could there be to regret? How could there not be wild bounty? What has no beginning continues whole and through to completion. Before every turning point, there are three transition days. After every turning point, there are three transition days. And then good fortune prevails.

6

Reverence beneath reverence. Lose that resting place where you use an ax to establish the rich comforts of home, and calamity will be inexhaustible indeed.

58

OPENING

Penetrating everywhere, opening is inexhaustible in bringing forth wild bounty.

PRESENTATION

Opening is the same as delight. At the abiding center, it's steely as a mountain in cloud; and beyond, it's all tender assent.

Use delight, and you bring forth wild bounty inexhaustible indeed. Use it, and you move yielding and devoted as a river in following heaven and concurring with humankind.

Use delight to put the people first, and the people won't mind all that toil. Use it to battle difficulty, and the people won't even mind death. The vastness of delight: that, that is what inspires people!

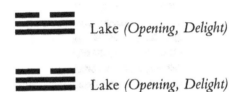

Lake *(Opening, Delight)*

Lake *(Opening, Delight)*

IMAGE

A lake's radiance and beauty: that is *Opening*. Using it, the noble-minded teach friends and learn from them.

LINES

I

Make accord your opening, and good fortune prevails.

2

Make the dedication of a bird sitting on eggs your opening, and good fortune prevails. What could there be to regret?

3

Make arrival your opening, and calamity can't be far away.

4

Make talk your opening, and you'll find no peace. Value anxious longing, and you'll know joy.

5

Strip it all away with the dedication of a bird sitting on eggs, and you'll know affliction.

6

Make a guide your opening, and you'll . . .

DIFFUSION

Diffusion penetrates everywhere, like an emperor staying close to the temple. Crossing a great river brings forth wild bounty, wild and inexhaustible bounty.

PRESENTATION

Diffusion penetrates everywhere. If you come steely as a mountain in cloud, you are never exhausted. In tender assent, you occupy a potent place beyond and in agreement with everything above.

An emperor staying close to the temple is an emperor inhabiting the abiding center of things.

Crossing a great river brings forth wild bounty. Riding the reverent and inward tree of wind across: that is where great achievement begins.

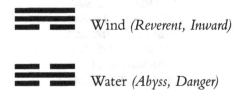

Wind *(Reverent, Inward)*

Water *(Abyss, Danger)*

IMAGE

Wind moving across water: that is *Diffusion*. Using it, the first emperors penetrated everywhere building temples and offering sacrifices to the Celestial Lord.

LINES

1

It takes the strength of a horse to raise things up, but good fortune follows.

2

Diffusion hurries in the loom of origins. What could there be to regret?

3

Diffusion perfects self. Then, you can live free of regret.

4

Diffusion perfects community. It's the very origin of good fortune. In diffusion there are hills and everything strangers and foreigners might think.

5

Diffusion floods through your vast cries. A true emperor dwells in diffusion, and so never goes astray.

6

Diffusion perfects blood. Then, you can leave to emerge through distances. How could you ever go astray?

PATTERN

Pattern penetrates everywhere. But a bitter pattern won't be inexhaustible.

PRESENTATION

Pattern penetrates everywhere. Tender assent, steely as a mountain in cloud: the two separate, and steely as a mountain in cloud moves to the abiding center of things.

A bitter pattern won't be inexhaustible, because its Way is soon exhausted and lost.

To navigate danger, use delight. To occupy your own potent place, use pattern. To dwell centered at the hinge of things, use understanding opening through it all.

Heaven and earth are made of pattern, and so the four seasons come to completion. If you establish laws using that same pattern, you won't wound prosperity or injure the people.

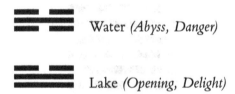 Water *(Abyss, Danger)*

Lake *(Opening, Delight)*

IMAGE

Above a lake, water: that is *Pattern*. Using it, the noble-minded can establish the various laws. Using it, they can move with deliberation and heart-sight clarity.

LINES

1

Never leave your door and courtyard, and you never go astray.

2

Never leave your gate and courtyard, and calamity can't be far away.

3

There's no pattern to follow. You may sigh in bitter despair, but you never go astray.

4

The pattern is tranquil, so it penetrates everywhere.

5

The pattern is sweet, so good fortune prevails. Setting out, go in veneration.

6

The pattern is bitter, so inexhaustible calamity can't be far away. Still, what could there be to regret?

CENTERED IN DEDICATION

If you are centered in dedication, the dedication of a bird sitting on eggs, even your simplest offerings of pig or fish will bring good fortune. Crossing a great river brings forth wild bounty, wild and inexhaustible bounty.

PRESENTATION

Centered in dedication is tender assent inside and, at the abiding center, steely as a mountain in cloud.

Opening and delight, reverent and inward: that is the dedication of a bird sitting on eggs. With that dedication, you can transform the nation.

Even your simplest offerings of pig or fish will bring good fortune, because your sincerity includes the simplest things like pigs and fish.

Crossing a great river brings forth wild bounty. Riding the reverent and inward tree of wind across, you ride an empty boat.

Centered in dedication, you know wild bounty inexhaustible indeed, and you move always in concurrence with heaven.

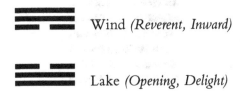 Wind *(Reverent, Inward)*

Lake *(Opening, Delight)*

IMAGE

Above a lake, wind: that is *Centered in Dedication*. Using it, the noble-minded deliberate over court cases and rarely issue a death sentence.

LINES

1

Always be prepared, and you'll know good fortune. Depend on empty gestures and mere artifice, and you'll know no rest.

2

Cranes are calling from river shadows, their young calling back. I have nice wine in bird-guise cups. Come, I'll share it with you.

3

With intimate companions, you must sometimes drum up enthusiasm and sometimes stay quiet, sometimes weep and sometimes sing.

4

After a few full moons, a horse loses its mate. Nothing goes astray.

5

Cultivate the dedication of a bird sitting on eggs. It's like silk thread and words and work. It ties you to things. How could you ever go astray?

6

The cry of a pheasant in flight reaches heaven. Calamity will be inexhaustible indeed.

SMALL BEYOND

Penetrating everywhere, small beyond is inexhaustible in bringing forth wild bounty. It's capable of life's small work, but not capable of life's vast work. A bird in flight leaves its cry behind. Don't live in accord with the lofty, live in accord with the lowly. Then vast good fortune will prevail.

PRESENTATION

Small Beyond is everything small living beyond, and so *penetrating everywhere*. Using that beyond, you'll be *inexhaustible in bringing forth wild bounty*, and you'll move according to your proper seasons.

Tender assent at the abiding center of things: use it, and life's small work will bring good fortune indeed. Steely as a mountain in cloud means far from the abiding center of things, your potent place lost: use it, and you'll fail in life's vast work.

The image of a bird in flight appears here: *A bird in flight leaves its cry behind. Don't live in accord with the lofty, live in accord with the lowly. Then vast good fortune will prevail.* Ignore the lofty, and follow the lowly yielding and devoted as a river.

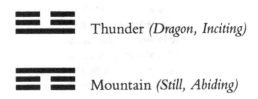 Thunder *(Dragon, Inciting)*

Mountain *(Still, Abiding)*

IMAGE

Above mountains, thunder: that is *Small Beyond.* Using it, the noble-minded move beyond veneration in their actions, beyond grief in their losses, beyond economy in their expenditures.

LINES

1

Act like a bird in flight, and calamity will soon come.

2

Move beyond male ancestors, and meet female ancestors. Avoid rulers. Meet their sage-advisors instead. How could you go astray?

3

If you don't move beyond merely protecting them, someone may come later and kill them. Then calamity will prevail.

4

Nothing goes astray. Don't move beyond them, meet them. Setting out against affliction, guard caution. Don't rely on the perennial and inexhaustible.

5

Laden clouds bring no rain. They drift away past our fertility altars in the west. Dukes carry bows and arrows, hunting things in the grave.

6

Don't meet them, move beyond them. But act like a bird in flight far away from them, and calamity will soon come. This is called *disaster made of foolishness.*

SAFE CROSSING

Safe crossing penetrating everywhere in the smallest ways: it's inexhaustible in bringing forth wild bounty. Everything begins in such good fortune, though it ends in ruin.

PRESENTATION

Safe crossing penetrating everywhere: it's everything small penetrating everywhere.

Inexhaustible in bringing forth wild bounty. Steely as a mountain in cloud, tender assent: when they both meet at the hinge of things, you occupy a potent place.

Everything begins in such good fortune. There, tender assent inhabits the abiding center of things.

Everything ends still and abiding, and finally *in ruin*, its Way lost and exhausted.

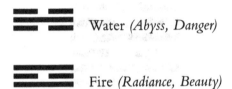 Water *(Abyss, Danger)*

Fire *(Radiance, Beauty)*

IMAGE

Water flowing above fire: that is *Safe Crossing*. Using it, the noble-minded anticipate trouble, prepare and protect against disaster.

LINES

I

Hauling wheels through, tail underwater: and still, you haven't gone astray.

2

A woman loses her headdress, but doesn't go looking for it. In seven days, she finds it.

3

When our exalted ancestor invaded the land of demons, it took him three whole years to conquer it. Don't rely on small-minded people.

4

In robes of fine silk gauze, there are robes of rags. Guard caution all day long.

5

An eastern neighbor sacrificing a fine ox may not compare to a western neighbor offering a simple spring sacrifice of wildflowers. It's sincerity that brings joy and prosperity.

6

Head underwater: affliction has come.

FAILED CROSSING

Failed crossing penetrating everywhere in the smallest ways: it's a fox foundering midstream, tail underwater. There's wild bounty in having no destination.

PRESENTATION

Failed crossing penetrating everywhere in the smallest ways: it's tender assent caught at the abiding center of things. *A fox foundering midstream* fails to leave the abiding center of things behind.

Tail underwater. There's wild bounty in having no destination. You won't make it all the way through to the end.

Steely as a mountain in cloud, tender assent: although they don't occupy their potent places, they move in concurrence.

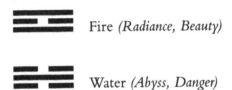

64

Fire *(Radiance, Beauty)*

Water *(Abyss, Danger)*

IMAGE

Fire burning above water: that is *Failed Crossing*. Using it, the noble-minded take great care to accurately explain the things of this world, and so dwell in their native land.

LINES

1

Tail underwater. It will be a difficult journey indeed.

2

Hauling wheels through, you'll know inexhaustible good fortune.

3

Begin an invasion with a failed crossing, and calamity has come. Crossing a great river brings forth wild bounty.

4

Knowing how inexhaustible good fortune is, you regret nothing. Sending thunder to invade the land of demons: after three years, his reward was a vast nation.

5

Knowing how inexhaustible good fortune is, you live free of regret. Such is the radiance of the noble-minded. And if you possess the dedication of a bird sitting on eggs, you know good fortune.

6

If you drink wine with the dedication of a bird sitting on eggs, you never go astray. But even possessing the dedication of a bird sitting on eggs—if you founder, head underwater, you lose this in which.

NOTES

vii *Root-Breath and Lady She-Voice*: Fu Hsi and Nü Kua.

2–4 *Heaven . . . Earth*: See Introduction, pp. ix–xi.

  2 *dragon*: The dragon is feared and revered as the embodiment of change. Winter comes when it retires underwater to hibernate, and spring comes when it rouses again and rises into the sky. See also Introduction, p. vii.

  2 *Way*: Tao, see Introduction, pp. xii–xiii.

  2 *hinge of things*: Cheng (正) becomes a key philosophical term in Confucius, where it means "rectify," as in his principle of the rectification of names. This translation tries to get at a more primitive conceptual level, where "rectification" suggests returning to the "hinge of things."

  4 *heart-sight clarity*: Te (德) becomes a key philosophical term in early Taoist and Confucian thought, where it translates as "integrity." In fact, it is the *Te* of the *Tao Te Ching*: *The Classic of Way and Integrity*. There it means "Integrity to Way," in the sense of "abiding by the Way," or "enacting the Way." Here in the *I Ching*, a deeper etymological translation seems more appropriate.

  6 *tender assent . . . steely as a mountain in cloud*: These phrases recur often (translating 柔 and 剛), sometimes referring to *yin* and *yang* hexagram lines respectively, sometimes referring to *yin* and *yang* as the cosmic principles those lines represent: *yin* and *yang*. And often, they refer to both together.

  8 *shaman-flower sticks*: Dried yarrow stalks traditionally used for consulting the *I Ching*.

13 *inevitable unfurling of things*: 命 in its more philosophical sense (it also means simply "command" or "mandate," as in the Mandate of Heaven described on p. ix) is usually translated "fate" or "destiny." But such concepts imply that events are *predestined* by some kind of fate or outside force. In the Taoist cosmology of the *I Ching*, with its perennially generative present, events are "destined" only in the sense that the ten thousand things unfold according to their own nature.

19 *grain of things*: The common meaning for 文 is civilized, cultivated, elegant, etc. But this meaning derives from an older and deeper concept that seems more applicable in the *I Ching* world: the ripples and streaks in rock or seashells, wood or water. Or, in the largest sense, the patterns of the Cosmos: such things as the patterns of stars, seasons, life and death, the diverse array of the ten thousand things. Hence, the patterns of

civilization are an integral part of the patterns of the Cosmos. And so, "the grain of things."

22 *yang . . . yin*: The two complementary cosmic principles, male and female, whose dynamic interaction produces the process of change.

22 *within . . . without*: In addition to their literal meanings, within and without can refer to the bottom and top trigram respectively.

28 *Presence*: In Taoist thought, Presence became a foundational philosophical concept. Presence is simply the empirical universe, which the ancients described as the ten thousand living and nonliving things in constant transformation; and Absence is the generative emptiness from which this ever-changing realm of Presence perpetually emerges. This is a later concept, growing out of the generative cosmology of the *I Ching*, where it is explicitly suggested in the Contentment hexagram (in which contentment seems not unlike Absence), the one other appearance of the term *Presence* (p. 33). But as happened so often in the ever-evolving ways of reading the *I Ching*'s mysterious language, the book came to be read through this cosmological framework. Indeed, it had already happened with Wang Pi's seminal commentary, in the note to p. 48.

33 *Celestial Lord*: Shang Ti, the monotheistic deity of the Shang dynasty. See Introduction, p. ix.

35 *Emperor T'ai . . . Bowhand Mountain*: Bowhand Mountain is where the Chou nation was founded by Emperor T'ai, also known as Tan-fu (literally "True-Father"), who was the grandfather of Emperor Wen (see Introduction, p. x). The story is described in this passage from the *Book of Songs* (#272, "Sprawl"):

> *Then T'ai our true father*
> *went early on his horse,*
> *following the Wei River*
> *west to Bowhand Mountain,*
> *found Lady Shepherdess*
> *and with her shared roof.*
>
> *Chou plains rich and full,*
> *thistle-weed and bitter-root*
> *like honey-cake, he began*
> *planning. Tortoise shells*
> *said:* This place. This time.
> *And soon houses were built.*
>
> *He comforted and he settled*
> *his people on every side,*
> *laid out bounds and borders,*
> *shaped fields, sent farmers*
> *east and west, everywhere*
> *fashioning his project well.*
>
> *He called master builders,*
> *master teachers, bade them*
> *build houses, plumb-lines*

taut and true, bade them
lash timbers into a regal
temple ancestors will love.

We hauled earth in baskets,
crowds swarming, measuring,
packing it hard hunk, hunk,
scraping it clean ping, ping:
a hundred walls built so fast
no work-drum could keep up.

Soon outer gates stood firm,
outer gates looming up, lofty,
then inner gates stood firm,
inner gates regal and strong.
And soon the Earth Altar too,
where all our endeavors begin.

48 *Return*: See Introduction, pp. xiii–xiv.

48 *heart-mind*: In ancient China, there was no fundamental distinction between heart and
mind: the term 心 connotes all that we think of in the two concepts together. This
range of meaning often blends into the technical use of 心 in Taoism and Ch'an
Buddhism, where it means consciousness emptied of all content, or perhaps consciousness
as empty awareness. The recurring terms "empty mind" and "no-mind" emphasize
this meaning. And at this fundamental level, mind is nothing other than Absence (*wu*),
the pregnant emptiness from which all things are engendered (see note to p. 28). All
of this is already anticipated in this *I Ching* passage. See also Introduction, p. xv.

48 *In return itself, you can see the very heart-mind of all heaven and earth*: For more on this
remarkable sentence, see Introduction, pp. xiii–xiv. Here is the commentary on this line
written by Wang Pi (226–249 C.E.), a profound Taoist thinker and author of the most
influential commentary on the *I Ching*:

> *Return means turning back to the source-tissue, and that source-tissue is the very heart-*
> *mind of all heaven and earth itself. Whenever activity ceases, stillness begins; but there's*
> *no opposition between stillness and movement. Whenever words end, silence begins; but*
> *there's no opposition between silence and words. It's like this even if the vastness of all*
> *heaven and earth is rich with the ten thousand things, rich with the activity of thunder*
> *and the movement of wind as they sweep the ten thousand transformations turning*
> *through their seasons. The tranquility of Absence, that is the source-tissue. It's only*
> *because activity ceases for us in our everyday earthly lives that we can see the heart-*
> *mind of all heaven and earth. If Presence were the heart-mind of all heaven and earth,*
> *how could different kinds of things come to exist?*

55 *oracle-bones*: Flat tortoise plastrons (ventral shells) and ox scapulae that were incised
with questions and used in divination practices during the Shang dynasty.

62 *ch'i*: *Ch'i* is often described as the universal breath-force; but understood more fully, it is
a continuous generative source, the matter and energy of the Cosmos seen together as

a single breath-force surging though its perpetual transformations. *Yin* and *yang* are its complementary female and male principles, whose dynamic interaction produces the process of change.

71 *Ancestral Mother*: According to one legend, this Ancestral Mother was essentially Lady She-Voice, who gave birth to humankind, for whom see Introduction, p. vii.

72 *Emperor Wen*: Wen ("cultured") is the legendary emperor who set the stage for the overthrow of the Shang dynasty by his son Emperor Wu ("martial"). He is also, according to legend, author of the earliest linguistic levels of the *I Ching*. See Introduction, p. x.

72 *Lord Winnow*: Lord Winnow (Chi) was an advisor to the last Shang dynasty emperor, who was notoriously tyrannical. For his sage advice, Winnow was thrown into prison. After the Chou replaced the Shang, Winnow became a valued advisor to the Chou emperor.

77 *lost horse*: This could also be the horse-star, which regularly disappears and then reappears. Hence: "Don't chase the lost horse-star: it will return on its own."

93 *Emperor T'ai . . . Bowhand Mountain*: See note to p. 35.

98 *emperors T'ang and Wu*: Celebrated emperors from early China. T'ang (regnant 1766–1753 B.C.E.) overthrew the Hsia dynasty, which had become corrupt and tyrannical, and founded the Shang dynasty. Wu (see Introduction, p. x) overthrew the Shang when it became tyrannical, founding the Chou.

100 *Cauldron*: A cauldron (鼎) was a huge bronze cooking pot often used for rituals. It had three or four legs, to hold the pot above a fire; "ears," which were handles for moving it; and metal rings on the lid to lift it off. Usually decorated with stylized animal motifs and text, cauldrons were an indicator of imperial power and authority.

102 *miles*: "Mile" translates *li*, which is about a third of a mile.

108 *A girl come home in marriage*: Represents the human incarnation of the generative moment in the cosmological process that drives all change: the intermingling of *yin* (female) and *yang* (male), earth and heaven.

HOW TO CONSULT THE *I CHING*

There are two methods for consulting the *I Ching*: using shaman-flower (筮) stalks or using coins. In either case, one approaches the procedure with some sense, whether vague or precise, of the question or issue to be addressed. Shaman-flower is the common yarrow (*Achillea millefolium*), and using it is quite complicated; but it is the original method and might be considered the only truly "accurate" method because the coin method produces results with substantially different probabilities. The coin method is by far the most commonly used, but some people prefer the shaman-flower method because of the tactile experience of using the stalks and because there is a meditative quality to performing its repetitive procedures. The shaman-flower procedure has evolved and changed over time, and its original version is not known. The version given here provides the essentials without superfluous details and seems best suited to the approach of this translation.

SHAMAN-FLOWER METHOD

Lay a bundle of fifty shaman-flower stalks in front of you. First set aside one stalk, which is not used. This is said by the early commentaries to represent the "Supreme Ultimate" (太極: *t'ai chi*), the generative Absence from which *yin* and *yang* arise, and all the ten thousand things in their perpetual transformation. The reason for this is because by setting this stalk aside you create an absence that allows the whole numerological procedure to work. Now, determining whether each line in the relevant hexagram is *yin* or *yang* (divided or solid) requires three operations with three steps each:

OPERATION 1

1. Divide the bundle approximately in half, to produce a *yin* bundle and a *yang* bundle. From the right-hand bundle take one stalk and place it on the table.
2. From the left-hand bundle, take away groups of four stalks until there are four or fewer remaining. Put these remaining stalks on the table beside the one stalk.
3. Do the same with the right-hand bundle.

Now, set the stalk from step 1 aside and count the stalks remaining. Mathematical principle dictates that there will be either 4 or 8 stalks. The numerical values for these are:

4 stalks = 3
8 stalks = 2

Write this number down. Then set these stalks aside with the "Supreme Ultimate" stalk from step 1.

OPERATION 2

Using the remaining stalks, repeat the procedure in Operation 1. However, after the three steps, do not set aside the stalk from step 1. Count all of the stalks. Again, the total will be 4 or 8. Translate them into the numerical value and write this number beside the first.

OPERATION 3

Repeat operation 2 and add the resulting number to the first two.

Now add the numbers obtained from the three operations. The total will be 6, 7, 8, or 9. These numbers translate as follows:

6 = old *yin*   —x—
7 = young *yang*   ———
8 = young *yin*   — —
9 = old *yang*   —x—

Young lines are strong and unchanging. But old lines are weak and in the process of changing into young lines of the opposite nature. That is, old *yin* becomes young *yang*, and old *yang* becomes young *yin*. This means the hexagram is in transition to another hexagram (see below for the implications of this). Draw this *yin* or *yang* line as the bottom line in the hexagram, and if it is an old line, mark it with an x through the middle.

Performing this entire procedure six times generates the six lines of the hexagram, from bottom to top. Once you have the six lines, find the hexagram by locating the upper and lower trigrams in the table on page 137, and follow the appropriate row and column to where they meet. That is the primary hexagram to consult by reading the initial Statement, the Presentation, and the Image commentary. If there are any old, changing lines, they are also especially relevant and should be consulted (though many consult all of the Line commentaries in any case). Then identify the hexagram created once those lines change to their opposites and consult that hexagram as well, for your situation is in flux toward the conditions addressed in that hexagram.

COIN METHOD

This much simpler method requires three coins, preferably Chinese bronze coins with a hole in the center. Whatever coin is used, identify a "head" side and a "tail" side. The "head" side is given a value of 3, and the "tail" side a value of 2. For each line of the hexagram (beginning at the bottom), the three coins are tossed and the numerical value of the three together tallied. The number will always be 6, 7, 8, or 9. After six tosses, the hexagram is determined. Then find the hexagram on page 137 and proceed as in the shaman-flower method.

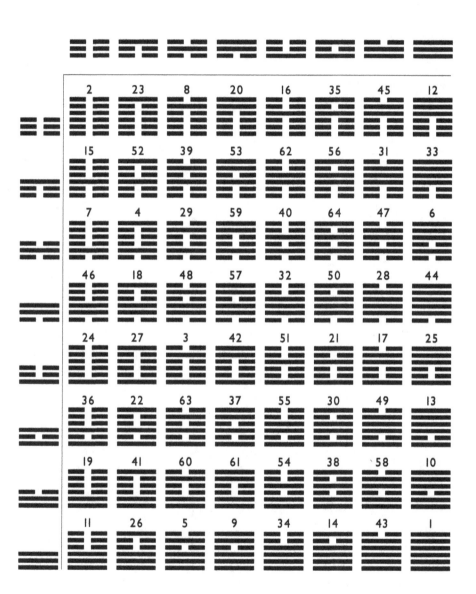